A COMPREHENSIVE
ROADMAP *to the*
COVERAGE YOU NEED

INSURANCE
Made Easy

TONY STEUER, CLU, LA, CPFFE

LIFE
INSURANCE
SAGE
PRESS

ALSO BY TONY STEUER, CLU, LA, CPFFE

Questions and Answers on Life Insurance: The Life Insurance Toolbook

The Questions and Answers on Life Insurance Workbook:
A Step-by-Step Guide to Simple Answers for Your Complex Questions

Secrets of the Life Insurance Industry Revealed:
Questions and Answers for the Right Coverage

The Questions and Answers on Disability Insurance Workbook

The Questions and Answers on Insurance Planner:
Be Ready for Life's Challenges

This publication is designed to provide accurate and authoritative information in regard to the subject matter covered. It is sold with the understanding that the publisher and author are not engaged in rendering legal, accounting, or other professional services. If legal advice or other expert assistance is required, the services of a competent professional should be sought.

Published by Life Insurance Sage Press
Alameda, CA
tonysteuer.com

Distributed by River Grove Books

Design and composition by Greenleaf Book Group
Cover design by Greenleaf Book Group

Cataloging-in-Publication data is available.

Print ISBN: 978-0-9845081-9-8

eBook ISBN: 978-0-692-02168-2

First Edition

This book is dedicated to my amazing wife, Cheryl, and my son, Avery. Cheryl's support and input have been incredibly insightful during the long process of writing a "mystery" book. Avery's humor and resilience in living with type 1 diabetes have been my inspiration, and he will always be my hero.

Bill Walsh is a legendary football coach and is considered possibly the greatest of all time. His coaching philosophy was innovative and went beyond performance on the field. Walsh called the following his "Standard of Performance":

1. Ferocious and intelligently applied work ethic directed at continual improvement.
2. Respect for everyone in the program and the work that they do.
3. Be committed to learning.
4. Demonstrate character and integrity.
5. Honor the connection between details and improvement.
6. Demonstrate loyalty.
7. Be willing to go the extra mile for the organization.
8. Put the team's welfare ahead of my own.
9. Maintain an abnormally high level of concentration and focus.
10. Make sacrifice and commitment the organization's trademark.

Contents

Introduction

"A winning effort begins with preparation."
—JOE GIBBS

I nsurance is protection against a potential risk. In the old days, if a house burned down in a small town, everyone in town would pitch in to rebuild the house. Insurance has now become infinitely more complex; however, the basic principle remains the same. Premiums are paid to an insurance company for a specific type of insurance coverage. The insurance company gathers premiums from many to pay the claims of a few. We all benefit from the law of large numbers. This necessary safeguard may be your household's largest monthly expense; however, it often remains a black hole of confusion. To understand insurance, you need to understand its purpose, what it does and does not do, and what you should expect from your insurance agent and insurance company.

I created the Insurance Bill of Rights to help consumers better understand their insurance and to provide a best practices roadmap for insurance agents and companies. My organization offers a seal of recognition: All holders of the Insurance Bill of Rights Seal—insurance agents, brokers, companies, and anyone involved in the distribution and servicing of insurance policies—agree to place the insurance consumers' interests first to the best of their ability and to follow the best practices in the Insurance Bill of Rights.

Insurance is full of jargon and confusing language, so I'll be using football terms to help bridge that gap and convey these concepts in more relatable terms. The best football teams are those where everyone is on the same page about how to play the game. On these teams, the coaches and players look out for each other, and the front office is open to feedback.

Optimally, your insurance team should work the same way—with you, your insurance agent, and the insurance company working together for your benefit. Although reading this book will probably not make insurance as fun as football, by the time you are finished, you will understand your insurance better. I encourage you to use the Insurance Bill of Rights to help you build and manage a winning insurance portfolio.

However, to succeed, you need to put yourself in charge. Take control by educating yourself and using that knowledge to obtain the appropriate insurance for your needs and to save on your insurance premiums. If you are faced with a devastating loss of life, health, income, home, or vehicle, having the right insurance in place can make a huge difference.

NAVIGATING THE PLAYING FIELD

Think of your insurance portfolio—all of your insurance policies—as your team. Building a winning football team is a challenging proposition, and insurance is no different. A good football owner understands that to have a winning season, you need the best managers, coaches, and players and have to understand the different positions on your team and how your players' skills interact. Not every player is a good fit for every team or a good fit for a certain strategy. Some coaches will center their team around a passing game or running game, while others will build off a strong defense. The best coaches build their teams around the players they have and then acquire players to fit the system they want. They then create a playbook to direct the players toward the team's overall strategy, so they know what to do in any circumstance. Your insurance strategy depends on your life stage and other demographics, such as your marital and employment status, as well as what you want from your insurance; each situation will require a different strategy. There is no one-size-fits-all winning strategy.

A roadmap allows everyone to be on the same page and to follow the same rules. This book, and particularly the Insurance Bill of Rights, is your roadmap. It will guide you through strategies for your particular needs.

Insurance agents are your coaches. You, the consumer, are in charge of selecting an agent for each type of coverage you will need, such as auto, disability, health, homeowner's, and life insurance. Sometimes you may have an agent handle multiple lines of coverage, just like coaches who oversee multiple positions. However, keep in mind that there are reasons teams have multiple coaches: It is hard for one person to be a specialist in all areas. Although some agents can certainly do so, they are few and far between. In this book, I'll show you how to choose the right coach for your needs and how to evaluate their performance.

The right insurance can make a big difference for you and those who depend on you. The secret to making this process pain-free is to take control by educating yourself and using that knowledge to save on your insurance premiums and obtain the right insurance to help you through a devastating loss to your income, health, home, auto, or life. If any of these are a risk to you, you need to insure that risk while also making sure you don't overpay for coverage you don't need.

It's time for you to step in and take charge of your insurance. You can do it by learning the rules through the Insurance Bill of Rights and then through mastering the process of choosing an insurance agent and an insurance company and evaluating different types of insurance. If you can understand the "fair catch" rules of football, you can understand insurance.

PART I

Getting Prepared for Your Insurance Season

"In football, like in life, you must learn to play within the rules of the game."
—HAYDEN FRY

CHAPTER 1

Playing by the Rules: Getting to Know the Insurance Bill of Rights

"Do right; do your best; treat others as you want to be treated."

—LOU HOLTZ

Football has a set of rules that every team and player must abide by. These rules are constant for every football game so that each team and each player knows what to expect and can be properly prepared. Imagine a game where each team had their own set of rules; it would be chaos. Football players and coaches are expected to follow not only the rule itself but also the spirit of the rule. The rules are taken seriously, and penalties occur when the rules are not followed.

Insurance works mostly the same way; there are rules that are consistent across the board, while there are other rules that vary by state, by insurance company, and even by how you purchase your insurance. The Insurance Bill of Rights provides an even playing field, with consistent rules for everyone—for consumers, for insurance agents, for insurance companies, and other members of the insurance industry.

The insurance industry is going through a historic transition due to access to information, stronger consumer laws, and advanced technology. With these changes, it is time to review and change how consumers and the insurance industry interact. It is time to protect the rights of consumers while defining the responsibilities for consumers and for members of the insurance industry. Doing so will have a positive impact for everyone involved at all levels of the insurance process, from reviewing insurance needs, purchasing an insurance product, and monitoring an insurance product, to making a claim.

Defining a clear set of unifying standards is how we'll create a roadmap for the insurance industry. The Insurance Bill of Rights will create a stronger relationship and a higher level of trust between consumers, insurance agents, insurance brokers, and insurance companies while helping sort out each party's responsibilities. The Insurance Bill of Rights is based on the simple premise that insurance agents, wholesalers, and companies should place the consumer's best interests first, to the best of their abilities. It provides simple, clear, and reasonable guidelines to accomplish this goal. This will set a standard of excellence for all in the insurance industry.

The Insurance Bill of Rights offers best practices. It was created specifically as a guide to what consumers can expect from insurance agents, insurance companies, and other members of the insurance industry. These best practices are intended to address many of the legal and ethical requirements applicable to insurance agents, brokers, and companies. In addition to these requirements, members of the insurance industry must also become familiar and comply with all other applicable laws and regulations.

The Insurance Bill of Rights also requires that members of the insurance industry act professionally. Professionalism here is defined by courtesy, honesty, responsibility, conduct, skill, good judgment, and a high level of excellence (going above and beyond what is required). If this is what we all strive for, then positive results are sure to follow.

OBJECTIVES

The Insurance Bill of Rights is intended to accomplish three major goals:

1. To strengthen consumer trust in the insurance industry

2. To provide a clear set of rules for insurance industry members

3. To improve the proper usage of insurance

Through effective, needs-based practices and fact-finding, it ensures that coverage is monitored to continue to meet your actual needs and encourages you to be insurance literate. For many years, insurance has been a black box, something that people know that they need but which they had no real, unbiased information about.

Because of this lack of information, most people do not have the right coverage to fit their needs. They end up with insurance they don't need, with premiums either they can't afford or they see no value in paying. It's time to change the conversation so that consumers end up with coverage that fits their actual need, with premiums they can afford. Monitoring an insurance policy and making adjustments over time to your insurance portfolio are almost always overlooked. Over the years, your insurance needs change. Sometimes the change in need is simple, such as getting a new car, while other times, it can be more complex, like when you have a new child who's not yet been added as a beneficiary to an existing life insurance policy.

This is where the Insurance Bill of Rights matters: Making these adjustments, just like performing regular maintenance on your car, is what will ensure that you have the right coverage when you need it.

Knowledge is power, and the power should be in the hands of the customer—you. Having and knowing your rights will protect and benefit you, and will call the insurance community to task, thus helping you and your agents optimize your insurance coverage and minimize your premiums.

Below are the ten rights you have under the Insurance Bill of Rights:

 The right to have your agent act in your best interest

 The right to receive customized coverage appropriate to your needs

The right to free choice

 The right to receive an answer to any question

 The right to pay a fair premium

 The right to be informed

 The right to be treated fairly and respectfully

 The right to full disclosure and updates

 The right to quality service and fair handling of claims

 The right to change or cancel your coverage and be notified of any change

This may seem complicated, but your rights boil down to the Golden Rule and general decency. Your insurance agent, broker, and company should be expected to treat you with respect and fairness and to communicate honestly and completely with you. You, in turn, have the obligation to do the same. We'll delve deeper into your rights in the rest of the chapter; look for the icon to see how each right relates to what you should expect from your insurance provider.

HOW DO I DETERMINE MY INSURANCE NEEDS?

Insurance is about defining your goals and needs; these are your foundation. And, yes, there is a difference: *Needs* are necessities and required. *Goals* are what you would like to have. Although there are commonalities

among certain life stages or types of insurance policies, there is no one-size-fits-all strategy; you will have your own specific needs.

You should discuss both your goals and your needs with your insurance agent to make sure they understand well enough to recommend the right policy (or policies) for you. Your potential coverage needs should be reviewed for each line of coverage under consideration, and your existing coverage should be taken into account. Any new recommended coverage must fill a specific need (i.e., a gap in your coverage). Any replacement must be carefully reviewed, with all pros and cons considered, and presented in writing by your agent.

How do I know how much insurance to buy?

Your objective in choosing coverage should be to meet your needs, but cost and reality sometimes dictate your choices as well. Keep in mind the adage that you don't want to be "insurance rich" and "cash poor." In other words, don't overextend yourself. While insurance may very well be needed, it won't do you much good if you must cut other necessities out of your budget. Balancing your overall financial needs should always be your primary concern. It's better to take less coverage to make sure that you can afford to pay the premium in the future.

QUICK GUIDE TO TERMS

- A *premium* is the amount paid by the insured (consumer) to an insurance company; this is usually monthly, quarterly, semi-annual, or annual.
- A *claim* is made by the insured (consumer) in the event of loss, damage, or other act requiring the insurance company to pay out a benefit.
- A *benefit* is the amount payable by the insurer (insurance company) to a claimant, assignee, or beneficiary under each coverage.

How can I match my insurance to my strategy?

Draft day is one of the most important days for a football team. Whether a draft is good or bad can make or break a team. Draft evaluation is something that takes countless hours for multiple members of a football team's home office. The best drafts occur when teams make smart decisions and base their drafts on the team's needs. Doing your own research and making your own judgment will keep you from drafting an underperformer.

In drafting insurance policies for your team, you will spend hundreds or, most likely, thousands of dollars a year, so you should make equally careful decisions. Consider spending at least as much time reviewing your insurance as you would selecting a new computer or television.

During a football season, many things will change. For instance, a player might not perform as expected, or they might get injured. The key to being successful is to remain flexible and to understand this state of constant change. Your insurance needs will continually change in the same way, especially with major life events, so it's important to review your needs at least every two years.

SHOULD I WORK WITH AN AGENT OR BROKER?

Having the right coach to meet your team philosophy is critical. If you are geared toward having a powerful running game but your coach invests heavily in wide receivers, you are not on the same page and will not be successful. Al Davis was the classic example of an owner who picked coaches based on the type of offense he liked to run. His most successful coach, John Madden, convinced him to modify his strategy, which led the Raiders to a 10-year winning average of 75.9% (regular games and playoffs), the second-highest winning percentage for any coach with over 100 wins. The bottom line: If you have a good coach, you should listen to him or her.

The key is for you to find a professional, qualified insurance agent who has exceeded the minimum requirements and who has dedicated themselves to being a competent insurance agent. If you are working with a professional, trained agent, they can provide you tremendous value—as much as any good coach. A qualified insurance agent, especially one who has taken the Insurance Bill of Rights pledge, can guide you through the process of reviewing your needs and selecting a policy, guiding you through underwriting to get a policy issued, and assisting you in continuing to monitor your coverage to ensure that you continue to have the coverage you need and to help you spot potential trouble with any existing coverage. When evaluating an agent, be sure to ask about his or her processes, which they will be readily able to explain.

Insurance agents will also know the insurance market—which companies are best for which type of product and, depending on the product, how different companies will view different health issues, which companies offer favorable rates for your area (for homeowner's coverage and related), and many other beneficial details that will save you time and money.

Why do I need a coaching staff and not just one coach?

Insurance agents and insurance companies tend to specialize in certain types of insurance. There are many types of insurance, and it would be challenging for anyone to keep up with all areas. That's why football teams have both a head coach and position coaches. The head coach knows the basics of each position, but they leave it to others to keep up with the specifics.

What is the role of my insurance agent?

Depending on the type of insurance you purchase, you will most likely be working with either an agent or a broker. Most insurance is sold through agents. An insurance agent represents an insurance company; a broker acts as an intermediary between an insurance company and a policy owner.

Are there different kinds of agents?

There are two main types of insurance agents. *Captive agents* are those who primarily represent one specific insurance company and who may receive office space and other support from that company. *Independent agents* represent multiple insurance companies and have more flexibility to find the optimal coverage for their clients at the most affordable premiums.

Is my insurance agent properly licensed?

Any person selling insurance must be licensed with the insurance department in the state where they work. Insurance agents are required to pass an exam administered by each state's department of insurance, as well as to enroll in continuing education courses on a regular basis.

Getting the license is trivial compared with those for most other professions. Pre-licensing requirements can include up to 40 hours of education in most states, while in other states, the number is lower or even nonexistent. There is no requirement of a college degree or specialized study of insurance.

Visit my website for links to the various state insurance departments. The resources and compliance standards may be more lax in some states than in others. On most state insurance department websites, you can research whether an insurance representative is licensed, and you may be able to view their continuing education, which will indicate their expertise.

What should I know about insurance designations?

Every industry has its own slew of designations, and it's always a challenge to determine which ones have any meaning. There are basically two types of designations for insurance:

Professional designations

Agents may earn professional designations, such as Chartered Life Underwriter (CLU) and Chartered Property Casualty Underwriter (CPCU). Agents who are also financial planners may carry such credentials as Chartered Financial Consultant (ChFC), Certified Financial Planner (CFP), or Personal Financial Specialist (CPA–PFS). These designations indicate that the agent has completed advanced training, passed rigorous exams, and is serious about professional development.

There are other designations that are meaningful. My website has a designation table with more information at https://tonysteuer.com/frm_display/insurance-designation-table/.

Rogue designations

Some designations are available to anyone who pays for them. These *for sale* or *rogue* designations can be earned through simplified courses over the Internet or by attending a weekend seminar. They do not require any level of in-depth study. However, they may be close enough in name to a professional designation or sound impressive enough to imply mastery of a certain subject. This has become a source of concern for US regulators and legislators. At the time of the writing of this book, this issue was being reviewed in depth, and some state insurance departments have banned some of the biggest offenders.

Your agent should demonstrate an awareness of their duties and responsibilities and know their limits. They should maintain a baseline of product knowledge, competence, and continuing education relevant to the insurance products they sell. For instance, if an agent is selling homeowner's insurance and all their continuing education is for life insurance, you should consider another option. Selling products they don't understand is an invitation to trouble for the agent and for you.

How do I choose an agent?

An important part of free choice is exercising it. In order to ensure your right to free choice with insurance, to choose the coverage that is right for you, you should seek multiple competitive options and choose your company, agent, and policy only after educating yourself. You should be fully aware of what you are purchasing. You should understand what the insurance covers and what it does not cover, along with all moving parts, fees, expenses, and risk charges—both projected and guaranteed.

Should I get a referral?

Referrals can be helpful, depending on the source. If your referral comes from a source knowledgeable about insurance—perhaps they're a CFP (Certified Financial Planner), CPA, or attorney—then their referral may be helpful. Keep in mind that even these trained professionals may not always have knowledge of specific insurance areas.

When interviewing prospective agents or brokers, ask at least the following questions:

- What is their established process for renewing policies?
- Do they act with reasonable care to make certain that policies stay in force?
- Do they follow up on overdue-premium notices?
- If something happens to jeopardize your coverage, do they give you adequate advanced notice of impending cancellation or nonrenewal, to allow you to maintain or secure alternate means of coverage?

Get to know your agent a little. Ask them questions to determine their values. Find out about their experiences. And ask if they have taken the pledge or follow the Insurance Bill of Rights. Do you trust this person, or do they seem overly eager to sell you coverage you don't need? Trust your gut. Remember, this is a relationship that may span many years and that involves a lot of your money.

HOW DO I CHOOSE AN INSURANCE COMPANY?

When choosing an insurance company, reviewing that company's execution and stability is crucial. Although you can switch companies easily with some types of insurance, there are other types of insurance where you are committed for the long term (think *decades*), such as life, long-term care, and disability insurance. Even if you are purchasing a type of insurance where you can easily move companies, such as with auto insurance, you need to choose a company that will actually pay a claim; they must have the resources and the service history that suggests they will do so. Therefore, a critical component of insurance planning is to choose your insurance company wisely.

How can I find insurance company ratings?

Don't get caught in the trap of simply comparing two companies and choosing the cheaper option. Instead, use a ratings agency and hold each company up to a predetermined set of benchmarks. Rating agencies evaluate insurance companies using specific criteria. The rating agencies assess a company's financial strength and its ability to meet its obligations to its policyholders. Fortunately, many of the leading sources of information make their ratings and analyses available to the online public, and almost all of it is free, although a couple of the rating services require that you register on their site.

There are four main rating agencies, and all four consider a company's financials, management stability, recent performance, and overall financial health, as well as external factors such as competition, diversification, and market presence. Insurance companies are not always rated by all four of the agencies, but a company with a top rating from at least three of the four agencies is in great standing. Visit my website for a chart that compares the ratings given by each agency.

- A.M. Best Company: http://www.ambest.com
- Standard & Poor's: https://www.standardandpoors.com
- Fitch: https://www.fitchratings.com
- Moody's: https://www.moodys.com

Financial strength ratings are useful, but a rating is not a guarantee of an insurer's financial strength or security. Selecting an insurance company is an exercise in common sense and research.

Finally, just because you're purchasing insurance from a top-rated company doesn't mean that it's going to cost you more. Since insurance companies generally have comparable expenses, reserve requirements, and overall investment strategies, buying from the best does not necessarily result in higher premiums.

How can I find out about an insurance company's complaint history?

Each state's department of insurance maintains data on the number of complaints against an insurance company, as well as pending class action lawsuits. To find your state department of insurance, go to the National Association of Insurance Commissioners (NAIC) website: http://www.naic.org.

You can also monitor your insurance company's reputation online. Do a simple web search for the name of the insurance company, coupled with phrases such as *claims, reviews, problems,* and *financial trouble*. You may also want to do a search on social media. This will provide you information that may not be reflected in the financial strength ratings or other financial information.

A web search for the insurance company name and *customer service* is also a good starting point. Do they receive positive customer satisfaction reviews? Visit their website and see how easy it is to contact them. Call their customer service number, which should be toll-free, to see what the wait time is, and ask the customer service representative a question about the coverage you are considering. Poor service means that you may not get your questions answered or your claims paid. Trust your instincts.

What if my insurance company fails or is moved to a run-off company?

Insurance companies have regulatory safeguards and financial guarantees. State insurance regulations place strict financial requirements on insurers that begin with very conservative accounting rules. Insurance companies are not only required to submit to regulatory reviews, but they must also submit to annual audits performed by outside auditing firms. Regulators also reserve the right to increase the frequency of reviews to a quarterly or even monthly basis if a company is deemed to be at risk of failure.

However, sometimes failure is inevitable. With issues such as prolonged low interest rates impacting various lines of insurance coverage, such as annuities, long-term care insurance, and life insurance, there has been an increase in run-off companies, which means that the insurance company has closed or been acquired and is no longer offering insurance. These companies will gradually wind up a block of business (or entire line of coverage) and cease underwriting any new coverage for that block. Since there are no new customers, the risk pool may deteriorate, leading to higher premiums or reduced performance. If you find yourself with a policy held in this way, consider whether you still need the coverage and whether there is a more solid alternative available to you in the marketplace.

In the event that regulators find your interests as a policyholder are at risk, they have the legal authority to order corrective actions in an effort to prevent or mitigate the impact of the insurance company's insolvency. Due to the level of monitoring, sudden failures of insurance companies are rare.

When a state determines that an insurer is insolvent, the mechanism used to protect its policyholders is the *guaranty association system*. All 50 states, the District of Columbia, and Puerto Rico have guaranty associations to which licensed life and health insurers must belong. State guaranty associations provide coverage, up to certain statutory limits, for resident policyholders of insolvent member insurers.

The National Organization of Life and Health Insurance Guaranty Associations (NOLHGA) is a voluntary association composed of the various life and health insurance guaranty associations. When an insolvency involves multiple states, NOLHGA assists its members in fulfilling their statutory obligations to policyholders.

The amount of coverage varies by state and by policy type. Current information can be found on the National Organization of Life and Health Insurance Guaranty Associations website, at http://www.nolhga.com.

TIP

Keep in mind that you have a responsibility to keep the policy in force even when an insurance company faces financial instability. If your policy lapses for nonpayment of premium or any other reason, you may no longer be covered through the guaranty association.

Has my insurance company taken the Insurance Bill of Rights pledge?

This is a new program, so an insurance company may not have yet had the opportunity to take the Insurance Bill of Rights pledge. To learn more and to read important tips on selecting the right agent and to download an agent research checklist, visit my website, and you can always use the Insurance Bill of Rights as your guide to selecting an agent and insurance company.

HOW DO I BUY INSURANCE?

The most important thing to remember during the application process is to fill out your application accurately and completely. Always answer questions truthfully and with as much background information as possible. It's better to err on the side of disclosure than not disclosing. If a question is not answered accurately, it may be grounds for the company to not pay benefits and to cancel coverage. Follow these steps in purchasing any type of insurance:

Gather information and apply

First, compile a list of all of your necessary information. For health, disability, life, and long-term care insurance, for example, you'll need your physician and medical group names. Be sure to include their contact information, dates consulted, and the purpose and outcome for each. Also include a list of all prescription and nonprescription medications that you take and their dosages; this information may be needed for the application, exam, or personal history interview. Other types of insurance will require similar relevant information, like your driver's license; your car's year, make, and model; and so on for auto insurance. Next, compile all required financial documentation, such as proof of income, then complete your application and any required forms. Most companies will offer conditional or limited coverage up to a set amount before the actual policy initiation date if you've evidenced insurability.

Submit your application to the insurance company for underwriting consideration. This will typically take four to six weeks, but it can take months if you're requesting a large amount of coverage or if you have, for example, a complex medical history.

Prepare for your physical

Most insurance companies require some type of paramedical exam during the application process for health, life, disability, or long-term care insurance; this usually consists of a height and weight check, a blood pressure check, and blood and urine specimens. The exam is often more comprehensive when you're older or applying for larger amounts of coverage and can include a more thorough exam by a medical doctor. You can find tips on preparing for your exam at https://www.tonysteuer.com. You'll also need to order your medical records, which could take three to four weeks to arrive, so plan accordingly. Non-health-related insurance won't require a physical.

Prepare for a personal history interview

This is a phone interview done through a third party that verifies information provided on the application and paramedical exam and additional questions from the underwriter. For auto insurance, your agent may have questions about your driving history. The company is making sure that all questions are answered consistently. Make sure you've got your ducks in a row on this one.

Complete any additional questionnaires

Additional questionnaires are often required for specific medical conditions and hazardous work-related activities and hobbies.

Brace for any modifications

Remember, there are thousands of factors that come into play—from illnesses and injuries such as lower-back issues or mild depression to whether you drive a motorcycle in a state with dangerous driving conditions. The insurance company may change some aspect of the coverage, such as a higher premium, if new information comes to light after your initial quote. Keep in mind that when applying for life insurance, the company may issue the policy with a rating (see chapter 7 for more information). Disability insurance may exclude some conditions from your policy. One or two exclusions or changes are not necessarily a reason to refuse the policy. This may not be a big deal at the end of the day; be sure to read it carefully and ask questions.

Make the final decision

After the underwriting steps are completed, either an offer of coverage will be made or coverage will be declined. If your application is modified or rejected, make sure it's crystal clear to you why you were not offered the coverage you specifically applied for. Sometimes, miscommunications regarding your health (e.g., inaccurate health records), finances, or occupation could hamper your acceptance.

Note that underwriters base their decisions on the information received, and they can sometimes change their decision when additional information is provided and reviewed. And remember that different companies treat some specific conditions differently, so your rate classification can vary from company to company. If you've been denied coverage, or if you're not happy with an offer, you should consider a second opinion.

HOW CAN I ENSURE I'M BEING TREATED WITH RESPECT, HONESTY, AND FAIRNESS?

Members of the insurance industry should always act professionally, in a manner that demonstrates professional conduct and the use of best practices such as the Insurance Bill of Rights. You need to find an agent and company with principles, values, and core ideals and who will act in your best interest. If you read through Coach Bill Walsh's "Standard of Performance," you'll find that it is essentially the Insurance Bill of Rights for football. The core principles of both are treating others fairly while working hard and doing your job as well as you can.

It is important to understand that an insurance agent is an agent of the insurance company and, as such, has a dual responsibility to the insurance company and to the policy owner. In working with an insurance agent, you should be clear on what the agent can do and cannot do.

What can I reasonably expect from my insurance agent?

Agents should abide by professional standards of conduct and ethics required by law through regulation, by their company, and by all applicable organizations of which they are a member, along with the Insurance Bill of Rights. Agents who have taken the Insurance Bill of Rights pledge show their commitment to professionalism and competency. The pledge requires that they have a minimum level of experience, education, and community involvement and that their conduct is ethical and beneficial to the consumer.

What should I know about conflicts of interest?

As an insurance consumer, you should be treated impartially and objectively. Agent and insurance company conduct must be free from competing self-interest, prejudice, and favoritism.

Insurance policies are, for the most part, sold on a commission basis. *Commissions* are the part of an insurance premium paid by the insurer to an agent or broker for their services in procuring and servicing an insurance policy. Certain types of coverage may include *no-load* or *low-load* policies, which are commission free. However, they only constitute a very small percentage of overall insurance policy sales. So keep in mind that your insurance agent, your coach, is going to receive compensation (cash or otherwise) based on the policy premium, the overall premium volume, and possibly the persistency or profitability of those policies. The cost of this compensation may be directly or indirectly reflected in the premium or fee for this product. This compensation is usually from the insurance company or from entities through which policies are written.

For example, if an agent charges a fee for designing a plan and then accepts a commission for the sale of a life insurance policy, you're paying twice for the same work. In this scenario, some agents will refund the planning fee.

California prohibits a life and disability insurance analyst (someone allowed to charge a fee) from receiving a fee and commission from the same client, and other states have similar rules. An agent's recommendation should not be influenced by commissions, bonuses, or other incentives (cash or noncash), and the agent should not collect both a fee and a commission from the same client for the same work. This would be considered a conflict of interest and should be avoided. The agent should disclose and mitigate any potential conflict of interest. If you see that you're being charged both a fee and a commission, you should consider finding another agent.

If your agent receives a fee, they should, at minimum, put the following in writing:

- The services to be provided
- The agent and client responsibility
- The duration of the agreement
- Any other relevant information

It is incumbent on your agent to also review the insurance code for your state to ensure they are meeting all requirements for the agreement.

However, conflicts of interest may be unavoidable, and the agent should identify these conflicts when they do arise and should have policies and procedures for overseeing and managing them, including where they may be self-dealing—taking advantage of their position to profit by selling you coverage you don't need, overcharging, or some other means. Unavoidable conflicts of interest must be disclosed to you in writing and should be managed in your best interests. The conflict is then explained, and you will be asked for informed written consent.

How can I ensure honest communication with my agent or company?

Your insurance agent and company should be truthful in communications and conduct and should act with integrity. Agents have a responsibility to take ownership of the decisions, advice, and consequences of their actions—or lack of actions. When your agent makes an error or an omission, they should communicate it to you and to the insurance company and then act to correct the issue. If the agent doesn't know something, they should admit it. They should either volunteer to research it themselves or suggest you find a specialist for that area.

Your strategy needs to be presented in writing; complete, clear, and truthful communication is crucial. Misleading communications, usually banned by state insurance regulations, can omit important facts or information or include facts and information that imply something that is either not true or not accurate. Be sure to read and understand your agreement.

Having a custom strategy and recommendation will form a foundation to communicate meaningful and responsive solutions. This increases the likelihood that a policy will be the best fit for you and will provide optimal value. It will be coverage that remains in force, which is a benefit for you, your agent (or broker), and the insurance company—a win all the way around.

Agents, brokers, and companies must inform you in simple language of your coverage options when you apply for an insurance policy. You have the right to know how each option affects your premium and coverage. Your different options should be presented with clear explanations of how these factors fit your needs and goals and how they can be changed to affect the premium. Here are specific factors that should be covered to provide you with free choice:

- The insurance product being recommended
- The coverage type
- The coverage amount

- Your deductible, copays, coinsurance, and waiting period (if applicable)
- Riders
- Premium payment mode
- What contractual provisions can be changed
- The pricing for all policy components
- Whether premiums are guaranteed or not and for how long
- Fees and expenses, dividends, insurance costs, and all other policy components that may be under the company's control
- Surrender charges (early withdrawal penalties)

Ask lots of questions. The answers should fully and completely address your questions and be understandable. If you don't understand something, you as the buyer have a duty to keep asking questions until you do understand. If you still don't, you shouldn't buy that policy. You have the right to all this information, and educating yourself on each item and how they affect your costs and coverage will ensure that you have the insurance you need.

How can I ensure I'm being treated fairly?

An insurance company owes a duty to charge a fair and reasonable premium. As we all know, not all of them do, and they may vary across different lines of insurance coverage. Some types of insurance have regulated rates, and some don't. This varies by state. For example, auto insurance and homeowner's insurance rate changes must almost always be approved by the state department of insurance.

Your right to quality service and fair handling of your claims includes the right to have your coverage needs reviewed at any time upon request, whenever a major event would impact coverage, and at least annually to determine if changes have occurred with your policy or in the marketplace that would dictate changes to the insurance coverage.

You also have the right to receive prompt, courteous, professional assistance, including on claims, and should be spoken to in a way that is easily understood. You should expect that all phone calls, emails, and other communications are responded to in a timely and professional manner.

How do I know if I'm receiving quality service?

Do your insurance agent or broker and insurance company provide annual summaries (statements) of coverage, and do they offer a way to review it with you? The following items should appear in an annual review of any insurance coverage. If you don't receive these items, ask for them.

- The insurance company's current name and contact information (any changes should be noted)
- The insurance company's financial strength rating
- Your policy number (if it has changed, this should be noted)
- Your coverage amount
- The type of coverage
- The current premium, along with any change from the prior year's premium
- A list of riders, with their respective premiums and dates they may terminate
- A list of discounts
- A policy termination date
- Surrender charges and periods, along with all fees and expenses
- The cash value and other policy values (if applicable)
- Your beneficiary designation (if applicable)
- Other policy changes
- In-force illustration to ensure that the policy is performing as expected (e.g., for life insurance)

How do I know if my claims are being handled fairly?

File a claim as soon as possible after an insured event occurs. A *claim* is a request for payment of a loss covered under your insurance policy. Be sure to review your policy so that you understand what is covered and what is not covered. Make sure that you file a logical claim, with as much documentation as possible by making a log, taking a photo, or anything else that will help you.

Keep in mind that insurance companies require you to mitigate your damages; in other words, you must take reasonable care to prevent further damage, such as turning off the power and gas if you can't stay in your home. Be sure to continue to pay your premiums while your claim is being processed.

To summarize your rights when it comes to filing claims, be aware of the following. You have the right to the prompt and fair handling of claims. You have the right to ask about any payments made to others by your company and charged to your policy. If your claim is denied, the company must provide you with a written explanation for the denial. You have the right to reject any settlement offer, including any unfair valuation, offered by the insurance company. If you reject a settlement offer, your options include continuing to negotiate with the insurer or pursuing legal remedies, such as mediation or filing a lawsuit. You have the right to not provide information that is not required to process your claim.

What if I have a complaint?

You can file a complaint with your state insurance department. With a variable insurance product, you may wish to file your complaint with FINRA or the SEC.

HOW CAN I MAKE SURE I KNOW WHAT I'M BUYING?

The rule that I use to test my own comprehension is to ensure that I understand the answer well enough that I can then explain it to someone else. Make sure you review all of the paperwork sent to you. You should be sure you understand what you're buying before you sign any agreement.

It is best for everyone if important information, especially disclosures, is put into writing. Clear and truthful communications are understandable to the average person, do not mislead, and ensure that everyone is on the same page.

Your agent and insurance company should follow industry best practices and the Insurance Bill of Rights. Be sure to use the following as a guide during any insurance purchasing and monitoring lifecycle:

Exercise your right to a free look period. When you receive your policy, review the policy to ensure that all information is accurate. The *declarations page*, sometimes known as the *data page*, will include the policy number, dollar amount of coverage, endorsements, and riders. The free look period allows you a certain amount of time to review the policy and be able to cancel it while receiving a full refund. The free look period will vary by coverage and state, so review it carefully so you don't get locked into a policy you don't want. Once the free look period is past, the policy may have surrender charges, early termination penalties, or other restrictions on the return of premiums.

The insurance company should provide you with written notices and statements regarding summaries of coverage. If you do not receive these, check with your company for online access and update the policy tracker provided on my website on the annual anniversary date of your policy. To access the policy tracker, visit my website.

You also have the right to receive reasonable notice of cancellation by the insurance company. Insurance companies can cancel a policy for nonpayment of premiums, and they do have an obligation to inform you as to why they are canceling a policy.

Are you asking enough questions?

Questions allow all parties to be clear on what type of insurance and how much coverage is appropriate, needed, and recommended. This helps to eliminate assumptions.

Is anyone taking notes?

All parties should make their own notes and documentation to include the date and names of all participants. Document all key decisions and directions.

Is there a written recap of a meeting?

Ideally, it should come from the agent, broker, or insurance company; however, you as the insurance consumer can also summarize any conversation and send it in an email. This puts it in writing and provides evidence for what was understood. Written follow-ups with summaries of conversations should end with a query for the other party to confirm the information. If the document indicates a certain number of pages, make sure you receive all the pages. If you are told a response or summary cannot be committed to in writing, that should be a huge red flag and a sign to walk away from that agent or company.

Was information added to the application or other paperwork after you signed it?

Always review all paperwork after you've been given your signed copy to ensure that no new information has been added. Agents and brokers can and do pre-complete applications, but they shouldn't change an agreement after you've signed the application.

How do I know if my insurance company made a requested change to my policy?

If a change has been requested, the insurance company should provide written proof that the change was made. For example, if you have submitted a request to change a beneficiary, make sure you receive written confirmation of this change; if you don't, it may be too late when it's time to file a claim.

What if my policy changes after I've purchased it?

You should be notified of any changes in your coverage and any relevant changes in the marketplace in easy-to-understand language. Providing full disclosure and updated information is simply doing the right thing. You should expect that your insurance agent (or broker) and insurance company provide the best information they can, and if you find that they are not doing so, you should replace them.

How do I determine the entire real cost of a policy?

Because life insurance policies are used as asset accumulation vehicles (despite that being a poor choice), it is important to determine their true cost. For you to make an informed decision, you must recognize that fees and expenses have a significant impact on premiums and, where applicable, on policy performance. Over the long term, even small fees can have a big impact on a policy's long-term cost. For starters, you should do all of the following to ensure that you're well informed:

- Review all documentation, including policies, quotes, and illustrations.
- Ask questions so that you understand how fees and expenses will impact your policy. Ask for a summary list of all fees and expenses.
- Review what discounts are available for the type of insurance you are reviewing.
- Ask your agent or broker how the fees and expenses on one policy compare with those of other policies.
- Be aware that there can be hidden costs. Monitor your policies from year to year and compare the information you receive. See if the net amount of premium changes, and look for changes in any other costs.
- Carefully read and reread all policies and contracts, and match them up with any proposals, illustrations, or quotes. If anything is different, missing, or difficult to understand, ask about it.
- Discuss with your agent or broker their commissions and how

they are determined, along with what other bonuses and incentives they will receive.

Privacy and confidentiality

Information must be treated by your insurance representatives as confidential, except as required in response to proper legal process. You have the right to expect that any information provided to members of the insurance industry will not be disclosed to others unless specifically authorized by you. This includes sharing it with their partners.

No pressure

You should not be pressured into buying a policy before you fully understand it and know it fits your needs. If you are given a deadline, you should ask the reason. Ask for time to think things over; a good deal will still be there tomorrow. This tactic works well if you're not sure about something. Inform your agent or broker that you need to go over your offer with someone else first (e.g., your spouse). If the insurance agent discourages you from this or says that it's a special deal, that's a big red flag.

WHAT IS UNDERWRITING?

Underwriting is a critical component of determining your final premium. It is a risk assessment performed when you apply for most types of insurance. Have your insurance agent or insurance company provide details on the underwriting process and the potential risk classification for what you are insuring. You should understand the process, which is specific to each type of insurance coverage. Your expectation should match the reality of underwriting: If you have major health issues, it will impact life insurance, while having a fancy sports car will impact your auto insurance rates. Common items reviewed during the underwriting process, depending on the type of coverage applied for, include the following:

- Your driving record
- Your public records
- Your Comprehensive Loss Underwriting Exchange (CLUE) report, a list of all claims you have filed

- Your credit history
- Medical records
- Lab test results
- Prescription drug histories
- Phone interviews
- Insurance exams

After the insurance company has your application and all of the underwriting requirements, they will make a decision on whether to offer coverage and at what premium. The more information the underwriter has, the more complete their understanding will be, and the more accurate their ability to properly price your risk will be.

What are modified offers, ratings, and exclusions?

Depending on the type of coverage, the premium may be higher (or lower) than your quoted premium. Coverage could be modified or offered with exclusions for certain issues, based on risk discovered during underwriting, or the company could decline the application.

A *modified offer* is when an insurance company offers coverage under different terms than those you applied for (e.g., a limited benefit period rather than a benefit to age 65 on a disability insurance policy).

A *rating* is when an insurance company feels that there is a need for a higher premium due to a specific condition or activity (e.g., skydiving).

An *exclusion* is a limitation for claims resulting from a specified condition or activity.

What happens once I hear back from underwriting?

Once an underwriting decision has been made, your policy will be issued, and you should be notified about the decision and the reason for any adjustments. You are under no obligation to accept an offer that does not match the original quote. However, you should consider the offer to see if it still meets your goals and provides leverage (premiums compared to total potential benefits). If you know the reason for the change, you may provide any additional information or context to the underwriter that might impact their decision. If you are working with an agent or broker, they should also review the information with other companies' underwriting criteria (and those companies' underwriting departments) to see if there are viable alternatives.

What if I don't like the offer?

Even if an offer is not what you expect, it is still an offer of coverage to protect against a certain risk. The risk still exists, so the question is whether the premium is reasonable and affordable. Insurance purchasers often get stuck at the fact that the offer does not match the original quote rather than accepting that it is simply a modified offer with different terms. A change in the offer is nothing personal.

I recommend the following strategy if you feel your offer is not great but it does meet your needs: Accept the policy and continue searching the marketplace. This strategy works better with some types of policies than others, and you should consider any cancelation penalties or surrender charges that may apply.

What if my application is rejected?

Insurance companies can refuse to offer you coverage based on nondiscriminatory reasons; however, they must identify the reasons for their denial in writing. This written statement must fully explain the decision, including the specific incidents, circumstances, or risk factors that resulted in the denial of coverage or modified extra premium.

HOW DO I MAXIMIZE THE VALUE OF MY INSURANCE?

There are many ways to save. Each insurance company has their own pricing strategy and can be more or less competitive in specific tiers. Companies also have different perspectives on medical and health issues.

To have a successful, winning insurance portfolio, you will need to pay premiums, which, in some cases, can seem high. *Premiums* are the amount paid to an insurer. The key with insurance premiums is to optimize your premium and coverage.

How is my premium calculated?

You have the right to pay a fair premium, including full disclosure on how the policy premiums are calculated and the impact of different risk factors specific to the type of coverage proposed. Your agent or company should also provide information on factors that may reduce or increase the premium in the future.

An insurance company may have multiple pricing components (variables) for a specific type of policy, and these pricing components should be disclosed to you. You then need to make sure that you understand them before signing an application or paying a premium.

Know what insurance companies can and cannot use in determining premiums. Discriminating by race, creed, religion, and similar factors is never allowed.

You have the right to receive a notice when your premium is due. However, some insurance companies do not send premium notices or may only be required to send them under certain guidelines—for example, just to seniors. Make sure that you set a reminder to pay your premium when it is due.

Companies develop their premiums using different systems; therefore, it may not always be easy to compare different quotes from different companies. The companies will use different factors and assign different weights to those factors. Your agent or insurance company will be able to help you with your questions. Again, it's important to look around and get multiple quotes.

How do I lower my premiums?

Your agent or broker and insurance company should work with you on strategies to reduce your premium outlay. Each insurance company will have their own discounts and other ways to reduce this. Here are some general strategies to keep in mind:

Review the options for your circumstances

Underwriting criteria varies by company. A certain issue may cause an increase with one company while another company will ignore it.

Discounts

The available discounts will vary by company. Be sure to ask about this when researching each company. To learn more, reference the chapters for each type of insurance.

Deductible

A *deductible* is the amount you must pay out of pocket on a claim before the policy pays. The general rule is the higher the premium, the lower the deductible. A higher deductible means that there is less risk to the insurance company and more risk to you, the insurance consumer. The reduction of risk to an insurance company typically results in a lower premium. But there is always an exception to the rule. See the following section on how to calculate your optimal deductible.

Proper coverage amount and type

Purchase only the insurance coverage that you need, and make certain that you are purchasing the right coverage to insure a specific risk, so that a claim will be paid when expected.

Reviewing riders and endorsements

These are add-ons to the basic policy that change the terms, conditions, or limits of coverage. Some can add value, however many of them are not worth the additional premium.

Premium mode

Changing how often you pay your premium could save you money. Usually you have a choice of whether to pay premiums monthly, quarterly, semiannually, or annually. Insurance companies typically charge extra when you pay other than annually. You typically pay an extra 2%–6% if you pay the premium twice a year, an extra 4%–20% if you pay quarterly, and so on.

Bundle policies with one company

Insurance companies that offer multiple types of policies will usually allow you to bundle or combine the policies. Depending on the company, this can include auto insurance, homeowner's insurance, umbrella (personal liability), life insurance, and specialty insurance such as for a motorcycle or boat. Make sure that the company you choose to bundle policies with has solid financial strength ratings. There are advantages and disadvantages to bundling policies, so be sure to consider whether the advantage of discounts, combined billing, and coordination of service outweighs the disadvantages of inertia (not shopping around) and premiums going up. Get quotes separately for each type of coverage and compare to the bundled premium.

How do I calculate the optimal deductible?

There is no set-in-stone formula for calculating your deductible; sometimes insurance companies will price in an "incentive" for a certain deductible, so doing a calculation manually is always a good idea. Ask yourself whether the money you save in insurance premiums justifies taking on a higher risk, along with a higher deductible (and with health insurance, higher copays and coinsurance).

Calculate the additional risk that you are taking on and divide it by the annual savings to determine your break-even point. For example, if you pay $1,200 a year to cover a vehicle and you can save $400 a year by increasing the deductible from $1,000 to $4,000, you are assuming an additional $3,000 of risk (out of pocket) in the event of an accident, for an annual savings on premiums of $400. $3,000 divided by $400 equals 7.5 years. Therefore, you would have to go 7.5 years to break even. Is that a reasonable risk?

For health insurance, you will also need to factor in your average annual copays and coinsurance for all health-related expenses. This does not include any tax savings through a health savings account.

To help you in your calculations, we have created the Optimal Deductible Calculator, available on my website.

What if I need to cancel my policy?

You have the right to cancel your insurance policy at any time. However, whether it makes sense to do so will depend on the type of policy. You may face a loss of unearned premium, surrender charge, or other withdrawal penalty. Be sure to review the monitoring section of the respective chapter for the specific type of insurance.

IT'S A TWO-WAY STREET: AVOIDING FRAUD

You should be respected by your agent, broker, or insurance company, but you should also treat them with respect. An environment of mutual respect leads to an atmosphere of trust, confidence, and excellence through mutual cooperation.

When dealing with insurance companies, the truth always comes out. Remember, with the Internet, checking accuracy on the facts you provide is relatively simple. You should always assume your information will be verified and give accurate information. Insurance companies review data from social networking and social media sites to combat fraud or misrepresentations by applicants and insured customers in paying claims. For example, if you have filed a disability claim and then post a picture of yourself running a marathon, your claim will be voided, and the insurance company will file fraud charges. Your contract also includes something called a *contestable period*—a period of time (usually the first two years) during which the insurance company can contest your policy. Try to gather all the necessary information before getting a quote, but if you don't know or can't remember a piece of information, don't make it up or guess.

This can range from a simple misstatement or overlooking something to purposefully omitting a critical piece of information. Beware of inaccuracies from guessing—don't guess! You should be certain or let the agent know that you're not. If you don't remember an exact date for an event such as a medical test, speeding ticket, or burglary, it's best to estimate (i.e., give the month instead of the date) or let the insurance company know it occurred and you can't remember when.

Insurance agents and insurance companies are only able to provide the best assistance and advice when you are completely honest with them. Providing accurate information from the outset will help you get the best quote, the one most likely to fit your actual needs and premium requirements.

What is insurance fraud?

Insurance fraud is the second most costly form of white-collar crime in the United States, according to the National Insurance Crime Bureau, costing billions of dollars a year. Insurance fraud is reflected in higher premiums. Insurance fraud can happen to anyone, and the key is often confusion.

There are two types of insurance fraud. The first is committed by a member of the insurance industry, including an agent, broker, or company. The second is insurance fraud committed by a consumer.

Always trust your instincts, and remember: If it sounds too good to be true, then it probably is. Keep in mind that I recommend only working with an insurance agent and insurance company that have received the Insurance Bill of Rights Seal.

For your own part, depending on the situation, lying, fraud, and dishonesty can, in the best-case scenario, result in your coverage being voided or adjusted. Lying to get a better rate can be tempting, but it does come with consequences you don't want to face. In a worst-case scenario, you may lose your coverage completely and may even go to jail.

There are two primary types of insurance fraud committed by policy owners as defined by the Coalition Against Insurance Fraud:

Soft insurance fraud

Soft crimes could be thought of as the "little white lies" of insurance fraud and might entail something such as falsely inflating damages related to a claim. An example of this could be claiming that several items were in your car at the time it was stolen, when these items weren't present—or in some instances, never existed in the first place.

Hard insurance fraud

Hard fraud represents a much more serious problem and involves something like deliberately faking or causing an accident, injury, or theft. This type of crime typically involves one or two individuals, although it has become increasingly common for hard insurance fraud to be perpetrated by organized crime rings.

While insurance fraud may be tempting or may not be considered a big deal, it's not good for anyone. If you expect your insurance companies to treat you fairly as a consumer, you need to treat the insurance companies the same way. In the end, the cost of insurance fraud is shouldered by other customers—those who do not commit the fraud—not the insurance company, and you may have no insurance when you make a claim, which could cost you thousands of dollars or even your life savings.

CHAPTER 2

Insurance for All Seasons: Choosing Your Strategy

*"Have a plan. Follow the plan, and you'll be surprised
how successful you can be. Most people don't have a plan.
That's why it's easy to beat most folks."*

—PAUL "BEAR" BRYANT, FOOTBALL COACH,
UNIVERSITY OF ALABAMA'S CRIMSON TIDE

Bear Bryant, at the time of his retirement, held the records for most wins as a college football head coach, having won six national championships. Bear is regarded as one of the true great coaches. His twenty-five-year career ran a long time; to be successful required Bear to plan ahead and be willing to make changes to his plans.

Life is the same way; our various life stages can last long periods, although they do change as you age. And as you age, your insurance needs will change. The best football teams are those who adapt. Football teams face many changes over time, especially considering how short players' careers can be and how frequent injuries occur. To maintain success, you have to constantly monitor your own team as well as the rest of the league and be ready to make a change to your roster when needed.

Insurance follows the same pattern. As our lives change and we enter new phases, our insurance needs will also change. There is also a need to monitor our insurance portfolios to ensure that our policies are still performing as needed and to assess if they've become "drop" candidates that require further action.

Insurance, contrary to traditional thinking, is not a "buy it and shelve it" product. There are many events that can cause your insurance needs to change. For example, getting a new job that requires you to drive many more miles each year could require an adjustment to your auto policy, while remodeling or starting a home-based business would most likely call for changes to your homeowner's policy. Having a baby or getting married means your health insurance needs will change. Even market changes, such as an increase in construction costs, could warrant an increase to your homeowner's coverage to maintain the same level of protection.

Regardless of which types of insurance you own now, your coverage is bound to require some adjustment over the years. You may even need to purchase new types of insurance that you didn't need before. Circumstances change, and you don't want to find yourself underinsured or paying for coverage you no longer need.

An annual insurance checkup is a smart idea. Considering what new types of coverage you might need and reviewing your current coverage once a year, even if you don't think there have been any significant changes in your circumstances, will help ensure that you stay adequately protected and avoid any unpleasant surprises if you ever have to file a claim.

To stay on track, do your annual review around the same time each year. For example, you could hold your review during your birthday month (to remember it easily), at the first of the year (to start the new year off on the right foot), or in September (when the kids go back to school). For health insurance and other employee benefits, make sure you know when your open enrollment period is (usually around October).

In addition to your routine annual insurance review, you should reevaluate your coverage any time there is a life event or significant change in your circumstances that either increases or decreases your risk—and, therefore, your need for protection.

In this chapter, we will cover many, if not most, of the common reasons for needing to adjust your insurance coverage. In some life stages, you will need to purchase increased or new coverage, while in others you could save some money by terminating certain insurance coverages. Because insurance needs and coverage terms vary from person to person, and coverage terms vary from company to company, state to state, and according to a household's individual circumstances, it's always best to consult with your insurance company or agent to make sure you've got the right types and amounts of coverage. The following are specific insurance considerations for major life stages. For each type of insurance, you can learn all about it in the chapter about that specific coverage.

WHAT ARE THE MAIN INSURANCE CONCERNS FOR THE COLLEGE YEARS?

Here are some quick tips for college students and parents to collectively consider at this life stage.

Auto insurance

You should check any current auto insurance policy. Ask about the rates for the college's city. This will help you decide whether to keep the car on the family policy or purchase an individual policy for the student.

Does the policy have a good student discount? If so, make sure that your insurance company is notified each semester (or when required by the insurance company) if your student maintains good grades. A good student discount will save you money by lowering your premium.

Health insurance

The Affordable Care Act allows parents to keep children on their health insurance plans until they turn 26. Most plans are through a certain health care system (Kaiser, Sutter, etc.) or through a network of medical providers that can often apply only within a limited geographical service area. Make sure that your student will be in the service network area. If not, they will have to pay significantly higher out-of-network charges.

Renter's or homeowner's insurance

Students usually own expensive and desirable items, such as computers, televisions, printers, cell phones, and jewelry, in addition to other belongings. For those who live in a dorm, most personal possessions are covered under their parents' homeowner's or renter's insurance policies. However, these policies often limit the amount of insurance for off-premises belongings to 10 percent of the total amount of coverage for personal possessions. Check your policy.

If the student lives off campus, it is unlikely that they would be covered by their parents' homeowner's (or renter's) policy. Parents should check whether their policy extends to off-campus living situations. A landlord's insurance policy does not provide coverage for a renter's personal belongings. Parents can sometimes add a special personal property floater or an endorsement to their homeowner's or renter's policy for specific items, or you can purchase stand-alone policies for computers and cell phones. You may also want to consider purchasing a separate individual policy specifically designed for students living away at college or a separate renter's insurance policy for your student. This can be a cost-effective way to provide insurance coverage for a variety of potential claim events.

Tuition insurance

In the event of a covered withdrawal, tuition insurance will provide reimbursement, up to the policy limits, for tuition, academic fees, room and board, and other eligible education-related expenses.

WHAT ARE THE MAIN INSURANCE CONCERNS WHEN I'M SINGLE WITH NO KIDS?

After you graduate from college or if you skip college, you'll enter the single years. (If you are married or have children, please move straight to that section.) Here's what to consider for this life stage:

Auto insurance

If you have been on your parents' auto insurance policy until now, it's time for you to take this responsibility on yourself. Auto insurance is required in almost every state, and you should at least have liability coverage.

Disability insurance

Once you start earning an income, you will need to protect it, so you can now consider adding disability insurance to your roster.

Health insurance

If you are still on your parents' health insurance plan, you should consider whether it makes sense to get your own policy. A big factor is where you live and if you have access to the network doctors and facilities. Going out of network will cost you a lot more. At age 26, you'll need to either get your own individual policy or be part of a group health insurance plan. You can purchase health insurance during the annual open enrollment period or when there is a qualifying event, such as losing coverage that you received through school, a job, or your parents. Graduating from college is not a qualifying event; therefore, you would need to wait for the next open or special enrollment period.

Homeowner's or renter's insurance

If you are renting, your landlord's insurance coverage will not cover your possessions (the contents of your rented apartment or house) in case of a fire or other event. Renter's insurance also helps you establish a favorable insurance track history (claims–loss history). This will help you with pricing and obtaining homeowner's insurance in the future.

Homeowner's insurance is almost always required by lenders when you apply for a home loan, and once you own a home, you will need homeowner's insurance. If you start off with a condo or co-op, it's important to note what is covered by the association; you will need to obtain your own separate policy for whatever is not covered.

WHAT IF I GET MARRIED OR ENTER A DOMESTIC PARTNERSHIP?

Insurance considerations change when two people are in a relationship and have reached a degree of financial dependency. Marriage, domestic partnership, and cohabitation require a commitment and changes in your overall financial strategy, specifically to your insurance planning. With some coverages, you may also need to choose between each person's insurance coverage. Reviewing the following will help you optimize your insurance coverage and minimize premiums:

Auto insurance

If you are married or have a domestic partner, you can qualify for discounts with most companies and will usually be viewed as lower risk. These discounts will vary from company to company. You can usually save by combining policies from separate insurance companies into one policy covering both cars.

Health insurance

You will most likely both have health insurance when you get married or enter into a domestic partnership. The issue is to decide which coverage to keep. Compare plans. Go beyond the premium, and consider what's covered, what's not covered, the type of plan such as an HMO or PPO, the network (your choice of doctors, hospitals, labs, pharmacies, and anything else important to you), deductibles, copays, coinsurance—and, yes, premiums do come into account. Be sure to include any stepchildren in your calculations.

Ensure that the plan you elect for both of you, if one of you does give up coverage, is one that you will be able to keep. For example, if you are planning to have children and one of you is leaving the workforce, he or she will lose their group insurance. In some cases, you may choose to keep both group plans if they are subsidized by your employers. For group insurance and health insurance (through the federal or state exchanges), marriage is considered a qualifying event, which means you can get coverage, even outside open enrollment. Marriages do need to be reported to your employer.

Home insurance

If one of you is moving into the other's home, be sure to add the new resident to the mortgage if possible, which will give both partners an insurable interest in the property. If this is not a good option, the person who is not listed on the mortgage will need a separate renter's insurance policy. Your engagement and wedding rings, along with other high-cost personal possessions, will need to be covered under your policy. Contact your insurance company to see if an endorsement or floater is needed. And if you are making renovations that will impact your home's replacement value, you will need to increase your coverage limits.

Life insurance

Many people mistakenly believe that they don't need to think about life insurance until they have children. However, marriage, a domestic partnership, or another form of combined household usually means that you each become financially dependent on the other person. It's important to ensure that your spouse or significant other could manage the mortgage or rent, ongoing bills, and debt if something were to happen to you. Remember that a nonworking spouse (or partner) provides an economic value to the household that would be expensive and time-consuming to replace, such as taking care of children, cooking food, and doing laundry. Be sure to update your beneficiary designations. This is often overlooked. You'll need to update all individual and group life insurance policies. If this is a second marriage, consider issues of children from a prior marriage; you may need new and separate coverage.

Long-term insurance

Spouses and domestic partners can usually receive a discount when both apply.

WHAT ABOUT WHEN I HAVE A CHILD?

Children will change your overall outlook and approach to life. Having children is also when most people really start to take a close look at their insurance planning. Here's what to think about:

Auto insurance

Having children will typically change your driving habits (and not just drive you crazy, which is a story for another book). You may be able to get related discounts for safe driving and for family cars, which will cost less to insure—think minivan vs. sports car. And your activities will now include driving children to daycare or school, activities, and friends' houses. Don't worry; even if you feel like a taxi, insurance companies will not treat you like a taxi for premium purposes.

Teenage drivers are another story. You'll need to consider adding your child as either an insured or as a listed driver. An insured driver will typically have more rights under an auto insurance policy. Adding a teenager to your auto insurance policy can significantly increase your auto insurance premiums.

Disability insurance

If you have put off getting disability insurance, reconsider it now. You now have an additional person dependent on your income.

Health insurance

Children are a qualifying event for group health insurance plans and federal and state exchange health insurance plans. Children need to be added to the policy so that they are covered, and this will increase your premium. For health insurance, you should contact your insurer (or whoever handles your health insurance) about adding your child during the pregnancy. There is typically a deadline for adding your newborn.

The rules for adding an adopted child are similar. Be sure to review your plan before you accept legal guardianship.

A special note for custodial grandparents: You can apply for grandchild coverage under Medicaid or your state children's insurance program. To see if you qualify, check with your state insurance department.

Life insurance

You will most likely want to increase your coverage, because your child is an additional person who is financially dependent on you.

Umbrella policy

Kids at play can result in injuries, and an umbrella policy will protect you if someone is injured on your property.

WHAT IF I GET DIVORCED?

Getting divorced has a significant impact on all aspects of your financial world, including insurance. Aside from the emotional challenges caused by a divorce, you do need to stay focused on what's important. Here are some of the things you need to keep in mind.

Auto insurance

If you and your spouse share an auto insurance policy, you will need to obtain separate policies. You will also lose the marital discount. It is important to remove a former spouse or other named insured from your auto insurance policy to protect each other from possible liability in the event of an accident.

Disability insurance

Disability insurance can sometimes be required as part of a divorce settlement, usually on a spouse who is required to make alimony or child support payments. The disability insurance protects the future payments. If a policy is required as part of your settlement, it is advisable to make it a separate policy, to ensure that benefits are clearly allocated. Some insurance companies will allow you to split one policy into two, so be sure to check with your insurance company. It is also recommended that the spouse or partner receiving the support be the policy owner and pay the premiums to ensure that the policy remains in force.

Health insurance

If you have separate health insurance policies, the only thing to do is to inform your insurance company of any new address. If you share a health insurance policy, you will need to obtain separate policies. Divorce is a qualifying event for health insurance, both through the Insurance Marketplace and under the Consolidated Omnibus Budget Reconciliation Act (COBRA). With COBRA, your divorce decree should cover who is going to pay the premiums and how they will be paid.

Home insurance

Your home insurance policy will need to be reviewed if one spouse or partner is staying in the current residence, especially because of changes to personal property.

Life insurance

Review whether you still need life insurance coverage. If you don't have any children, you probably don't need it, because there is no longer anyone financially dependent on you.

Life insurance can be required as part of a divorce settlement, usually on a spouse who is required to make alimony or child support payments, to protect the future payments. Term life insurance is a good fit, because the payments are usually required for a fixed period of years—for example, through a child's 21st birthday. If a policy is required as part of a settlement, it is advisable to make it a separate policy to ensure that it's clearly allocated. As with disability insurance, some insurance companies will allow you to split one policy into two, so be sure to ask your agent or insurance company. It is also recommended that the spouse or partner receiving the support be the policy owner and pay the premiums to ensure that the policy remains in force and the beneficiary is not changed. Be sure to change the beneficiaries on your policies, including any group life insurance.

Long-term care insurance

If you already have long-term care insurance, you just need to change your address. If you have a marital (or domestic partner) discount, it will usually not be removed.

WHAT ARE THE MAIN INSURANCE CONCERNS WHEN I HAVE AN EMPLOYER OR MOVE TO A NEW EMPLOYER?

Often the value of group insurance is overlooked or not understood. When you look at group insurance, consider the premiums paid as part of your overall compensation package, and consider that your employer would not be providing this insurance (and paying premiums) if there was not any value. Most employers do not understand or communicate the value, so it is up to you to optimize the value of your group insurance while you have it.

A new job may require other changes to your life, which will affect your overall financial plan and, specifically, your insurance needs. When you onboard, you have the big decision of opting in or out of this coverage. Most employers offer coverage through a cafeteria-style plan, where the employer gives you a certain amount of credit each month that you can use toward the types of insurance that you would like to have. Usually this credit ends up being a lot less than the total combined premiums of coverages that you may want.

Once a year, a strange phenomenon occurs that is known as *open enrollment*. For most employees, open enrollment is where they can practice the fine art of pretending that if you ignore something, it will go away. However, what most employees don't realize is that in this case, ignorance is certainly not bliss, and they are overlooking an important part of their overall financial plan that can have a dramatic impact on their future and the future of their family.

Auto insurance

If you drive to work, your monthly mileage will most likely increase, and this can affect your premiums with auto insurance policies that are priced based on usage (this is more common nowadays). If you use your vehicle while on the job, check whether your employer has liability coverage under their commercial policy.

Disability insurance

There are two types of disability insurance that you may have through your employer: short-term and long-term disability. If you are considering leaving your employer and you will not have disability insurance (either your employer doesn't offer it or you are starting your own business), you will usually only be able to get minimal individual disability income insurance coverage, because the insurance companies will require an earnings history of one to two years or proof of projected earnings, such as signed contracts. Obtain as much individual coverage as you can while you are still at your current employer, and purchase the maximum future purchase option rider. Because there is almost always a gap between group long-term disability and available individual coverage, you will at least have some disability insurance coverage in the future. The future purchase option will allow you to increase your coverage as your income grows without further evidence of medical insurability.

Health insurance

Prior to accepting a new job, compare your current health plan with plans offered by the prospective employer to be sure that you will have access to the most cost-effective mix of deductibles, copays, and coinsurance to meet your needs. You should also determine if your new employer has a waiting period before you receive the group health insurance coverage. If so, and you currently have a policy, you should keep it in force until your new coverage starts. If you leave your job, review your options under COBRA.

Dental insurance

If your employer offers dental coverage, it's worth looking at. If you're going to the dentist twice a year, this coverage usually makes sense, although it is usually limited.

Vision insurance

Vision insurance can usually be obtained for a low premium. If you wear glasses or use contacts, you can benefit from this coverage, although it is also limited.

Homeowner's insurance

If you are working from home and have office equipment such as a computer or printer, your employer's insurance coverage should cover these items. Commercial business activity is not covered under a standard homeowner's insurance policy.

If your job change includes a move, check with your homeowner's policy to make sure personal possessions are covered in transit. If they are not, consider a trip transit, moving, or floater policy.

Life insurance

Almost all employers offer group life insurance to their employees. Group life insurance coverage usually provides the amount of your annual salary up to a predetermined maximum amount of coverage. Often employers will also offer supplemental life insurance coverage in additional multiples of your annual salary. The basic coverage (multiple of salary) is paid for by the company and is *guaranteed issue*, meaning that the insured employee does not have to go through any sort of underwriting.

When the death benefit is paid, it is income tax free. However, any employer-paid coverage over $50,000 will be subject to income taxes for premiums paid. For example, if you have $100,000 of coverage, you would be subject to income taxes on $50,000 ($100,000 total coverage less $50,000). This coverage will have a premium that increases either annually or at five-year increments based on your age. The coverage will usually also terminate at your separation from the employer.

Supplemental life insurance is additional coverage that's usually purchased either in certain amounts (e.g., $25,000 increments) or by multiples of salary up to a certain dollar amount. This coverage is paid for by after-tax dollars, which results in an after-tax death benefit. This coverage is subject to underwriting (subject to medical history, etc.). Supplemental life insurance coverage is often portable; however, the premiums may change after you leave your employer. Employer coverage is usually more expensive than individual coverage over a long period.

Long-term care insurance

If you elect this coverage through an employer, make sure it is portable. Long-term care coverage is almost always portable; however, there may be a premium subsidy or increase if you leave your employer, so ask for and read the policy to avoid any surprises later on.

WHAT IF I AM SELF-EMPLOYED OR OWN MY OWN BUSINESS?

The big consideration here is whether you will have any employees. If it's just you, you should purchase insurance on your own and should consider your coverage needs and life stage (and of course amending for any individual circumstances).

If you have employees, you are taking on the role of employer and will want to consider whether to offer insurance benefits to your employees. What coverage you offer will be up to you (and your team). This may be a good time to reread the employee section.

The other factor besides employees that comes into play is your business's entity type: sole proprietor, partnership, limited liability company, corporation, or some other format. The entity type will often determine the type of plan and how it can be set up.

Insurance is a critical backbone of any business and can make it or break it. Even if you form a business entity to protect yourself from being personally liable for business debts and judgments, your business will not be protected against such things as fire, flood, and data theft. Running a business is not easy; however, you do need to protect yourself. You should strongly consider finding an agent who specializes in coverages for businesses of your size.

Following are the basic types of business insurance and other types of insurance to consider. Please keep in mind that these are general recommendations. Certain industries, occupations, and professions will have specific types of insurance that would be important to consider. For these types of coverages, you can review industry trade publications or websites for professional associations.

Auto insurance

You will need business auto insurance coverage for vehicles used for business purposes.

Business interruption insurance

Business interruption insurance provides coverage for the cost of relocating, paying employees, and paying rent if you have to move or shut down because of a fire or other event.

Business owner's policy

A business owner's policy (BOP) is a type of all-in-one insurance coverage created specifically for small businesses. These policies can be customized with a variety of configurations and coverage limits to meet your specific needs, including business income, liability, property protection, commercial auto insurance, and umbrella insurance.

Buy–sell insurance

Buy–sell insurance is obtained to fund a buy–sell agreement, made by the owners of a business to purchase the share of a disabled or deceased owner. The value of each owner's share of the business and the exact terms of the buying-and-selling process are established before death or the beginning of the disability.

Cyber insurance

Cyber insurance (also known as *cyber risk* or *cyber liability* insurance) provides coverage for recovery after a cybersecurity breach or similar event. There are no current standards; however, the typical policy will cover investigation, business losses, privacy and notification, and lawsuits and extortion.

Health insurance

Included in the Affordable Care Act is the Small Business Health Options Program (SHOP) Marketplace for small employers who want to provide health and dental insurance to their employees—affordably, flexibly, and conveniently. To use the SHOP Marketplace, your business or nonprofit organization must have 50 or fewer full-time equivalent employees. You don't have to wait for an open enrollment period; you can start offering SHOP insurance to your employees any time of year. You can also use SHOP even if it's just you. You can also qualify for a Small Business Health Care Tax Credit, worth up to 50 percent of your premium costs if you have fewer than 25 employees. Please note that this is optional, and if you have 50 or fewer employees you do not have to provide insurance. Visit https://www.healthcare.gov for more information.

If you have 50 or more employees, you must either offer a plan that meets certain minimum standards, including being affordable, or your company will be subject to the employer-shared responsibility provisions. This means you may owe a payment if at least one of your full-time employees enrolls in a plan through the Health Insurance Marketplace and receives a premium tax credit. The Internal Revenue Service offers detailed questions and answers about these provisions, including information on which employers may be liable for a payment, how the payment is calculated, and more, on irs.gov.

Homeowner's insurance and home-based businesses

Business equipment and materials associated with a home office or a home-based business may be covered by your basic homeowner's or renter's insurance policy. Ask your agent or broker.

Identity insurance

Identity insurance provides protection for businesses that suffer a data breach. It may also cover the costs of notifying and providing services to those who are victims of identity theft.

Key person insurance

Key person insurance is designed to protect your business against the loss of income resulting from the death or disability of a key employee. If you have an employee the business couldn't continue without, you may need this kind of coverage.

Liability insurance

Liability insurance provides coverage for your obligations and legal defense for accidents, injuries, and negligence. Home-based businesses also need liability coverage, since homeowner's policies do not provide protection against business liability risks.

Product liability insurance

Product liability insurance provides coverage for manufacturers, wholesalers, distributors, and resellers from being held liable if a product is unsafe or injures someone.

Professional liability

Professional liability (also known as *errors and omissions* insurance) provides coverage for service occupations such as attorneys, physicians, accountants, financial planners, and insurance agents from liability for negligence or malpractice in performing their professional duties.

Property insurance

Property insurance provides protection if your property is damaged or destroyed due to fire, storm, or theft. For a home-based business, your homeowner's policy may provide protection for your business property, or you may be able to add a rider rather than getting a separate policy. There are two forms of coverage: standard and special (which provides more comprehensive coverage than standard).

Umbrella insurance

Umbrella insurance provides additional coverage for losses that exceed the limits of other policies.

Worker's compensation

Worker's compensation provides coverage for lost wages and medical care for employees who are injured on the job. It is required in almost all states for employers who have more than a certain number of employees.

WHAT IF I SERVE IN THE MILITARY OR I AM A VETERAN?

Being part of the military, you will get offered numerous insurance benefits. Unfortunately, there are many people who try to take advantage of members of the military and their finances. Be sure you understand any insurance (or investment) offered before committing your money. You can find tips to protect yourself from insurance predators on my website.

Disability insurance

Disability insurance provides protection for injuries or diseases that were incurred in or aggravated during active duty, active duty for training, or inactive duty training. A disability can apply to physical conditions, such as a chronic knee condition, as well as mental health conditions, such as post-traumatic stress disorder (PTSD).

Disability compensation is a monthly tax-free benefit paid to veterans. The benefit amount is graduated according to the degree of the veteran's disability, on a scale from 10 percent to 100 percent (in increments of 10 percent). Members of the uniformed services are automatically enrolled, and there is no cost. Coverage extends to active duty, active duty for training, inactive duty training, or inactive duty training with the requirement that you were discharged under any condition other than dishonorable and that you are at least 10 percent disabled by an injury or disease that was incurred in or aggravated during active duty or active duty for training. If you were on inactive duty for training, the disability must have resulted from injury, heart attack, or stroke. You will also qualify if you are disabled after service, if the disability is related to the circumstances of service.

Note: Disability insurance is the only coverage that is not offered through the Office of Personnel Management. Instead, you get it through the US Department of Veterans Affairs. To learn more, visit: http://www.benefits.va.gov.

Health insurance

Under the Federal Employees Health Benefits (FEHB) Program, you have 11 or more health plans to choose from. These plans cover the range of health insurance types. Each plan provides comprehensive coverage for you, your spouse, and your children under age 26. Your service contributes to the premium. There are no waiting periods and no restrictions on preexisting conditions. FEHB has also started to offer self-plus-one coverage, which allows you to add a qualified person to your coverage.

Dental insurance

Dental coverage is paid for by the enrollee and is available for yourself, your spouse, and any unmarried dependent children under the age of 22 (including stepchildren). This plan is available with no preexisting condition limitations. Under the Federal Employees Dental and Vision Insurance Program (FEDVIP), there are currently 10 dental plans available, so you have a wide choice to find a plan that fits your goals. You can select vision, dental, both, or neither.

Vision insurance

Vision coverage is similar to dental: You pay for it and can elect coverage for yourself, your spouse, and any unmarried dependent children under age 22, with no preexisting condition limitations. Under the Federal Employees Dental and Vision Insurance Program (FEDVIP), there are currently four vision plans available.

Life insurance

The Federal Employees' Group Life Insurance Program (FEGLI) is the largest group term life insurance program in the world, with over four million people insured, which allows for very competitive premiums. FEGLI does not build up any cash value or paid-up value. FEGLI consists of basic life insurance and three options. New members of the military are automatically covered by the basic life insurance, and your payroll office deducts premiums from your paycheck unless you waive the coverage.

In addition to the basic, there are three forms of optional insurance, although you must have basic insurance in order to elect any of the options. Unlike basic coverage, enrollment in optional insurance is not automatic; you must take action to elect the options.

Your age does not affect the cost of basic insurance, and the cost is shared between you and the government. You pay two-thirds of the total cost, and the government pays one-third.

You pay the full cost of optional insurance, and the cost does depend on your age. The Office of Federal Employees' Group Life Insurance (OFEGLI), which is a private entity that has a contract with the federal government, processes and pays claims under the FEGLI Program.

Long-term care insurance

Long-term care coverage is offered through the Federal Long-Term Care Insurance Program (FLTCIP). You must apply for this coverage, which requires underwriting. For more information, visit https://www. ltcfeds.com.

Flexible spending account

A flexible spending account allows you to save money for health care expenses with a health care or limited expense health care account. These programs allow you to contribute pretax dollars to pay for expenses that are not covered through the FEHB, Vision, or Dental plans. A Dependent Care FSA is also available. These programs effectively offer you a discount by using pretax dollars. To learn more about the Federal Flexible Spending Account Program (FSAFEDS), visit https://www.fsafeds.com. To learn more about different types of FSAs, go to chapter 5.

For more information on official insurance programs for active members of the military and when you can enroll, visit https://www.opm.gov/insure. The website also has important information on how the life events featured earlier in this chapter are treated under the different insurance programs, so be sure you visit this valuable resource at https://www.opm.gov/healthcare-insurance/life-events/.

WHAT ABOUT WHEN I BECOME A SENIOR OR RETIRE?

Whether you retire from work, partially retire, or stay on, your financial perspective will change. You'll need to review your insurance portfolio to reflect your new stage in life.

Annuities

For the most part, annuities don't make good financial sense. In specific situations, especially for retirees, simple fixed immediate annuities can make sense for a portion of your overall assets (only a portion!). Annuities can provide a stable source of income, but they are not for everyone and can be extremely complex, with high fees and minimal liquidity. Anything beyond a simple fixed immediate annuity should be approached cautiously and is almost never advised.

Auto insurance

You may be eligible for some premium savings on your auto insurance. Adults between the ages of 50 to 70 are some of the safest drivers on the road. They have fewer accidents and usually drive safer cars. However, drivers over the age of 70 have higher rates of fatal crashes than any other age group except for teenagers. After age 70, your premiums will usually start to increase. Take a defensive driving course, because the majority of states require auto insurance companies to offer discounts to older adults—usually ages 55 and up—who complete these courses.

If you are retiring and have been commuting, your mileage will go down, which should reduce your premiums. If your coverage does not reflect usage-based pricing, now's a great time to review your auto insurance. If you intend to live in a different country for part of the year and will be renting or owning a car in those countries, you'll need international coverage, because this won't be covered under a traditional auto insurance policy.

Disability insurance

Your disability coverage will either terminate or the benefits will typically reduce to a two-year benefit period between ages 65 and 70 and to a one-year benefit after age 70 until whenever the policy terminates. You'll still be paying the same premium, but if you have sufficient assets already accumulated or you are not working, this is coverage you will no longer need.

Health insurance

Medicare is the federal government's health insurance program for those 65 and older. At age 65, you need to be sure to enroll during the specified period or face higher future premiums.

Homeowner's insurance

Check with your homeowner's insurance company to see if they offer a discount to retirees.

Life insurance

Life insurance is heavily marketed to senior citizens, with the implication that they should leave something for their children. That is not the point of life insurance, nor is it to pay for your final expenses. Life insurance is only to care for those who are dependent on you and can't earn a living or don't have access to other assets like retirement funds. In most cases, it doesn't make sense to keep a life insurance policy in retirement. It comes back to the basic question of your actual needs.

Long-term care insurance

Long-term care coverage helps with at least two activities of daily living such as bathing, eating, dressing, continence, mobility, and cognition in a wide-range of facilities, including skilled nursing facilities, nursing homes, and in-home care. Medicare does not provide any coverage for services covered under a long-term care policy.

Warning: Be wary of "senior expert" designations and elder fraud.

WHAT IF MY SPOUSE OR DOMESTIC PARTNER PASSES AWAY?

Being prepared for the death of a spouse or a domestic partner may not be a pleasant task. However, it is important and needs to be considered. If your spouse or domestic partner was employed, you should contact the employer's benefits administrator to ask about any benefits, which can include life insurance, unpaid salary and bonuses, accrued vacation and sick pay, leftover funds in a flexible savings or dependent care spending account, and stock options. You'll also want to check on any pension benefits and retirement plans. I strongly recommend getting more official copies of the death certificate than you think you will need (at least ten copies).

Following are some things to consider as you plan for, or respond to, this event.

Auto insurance

Contact your insurance company to have the deceased removed as an insured on the policy. If you have two cars, you'll most likely sell one, so you'll also need to terminate the auto insurance for the car once it is sold. Your insurance company will need to know which insured is deceased, if a vehicle has been sold, and if there will be any change in the type or amount of driving that will be done. When you contact your insurance company, be prepared with the policy number and a certified copy of the death certificate. This will impact your auto insurance premium, and you will lose the marital discount.

Disability insurance

If your spouse had an individual disability income insurance policy, it should be terminated. If premiums have been paid, you should request a pro rata refund of any unearned premiums. Some policies may have a small death benefit. Group disability insurance should be handled through your employer.

Health insurance

If you and your spouse have an individual health insurance policy, contact the insurance company to have your spouse removed as an insured. This will lower your premiums, so it's best to do this as soon as possible. If you have separate health insurance policies, you should terminate your spouse's policy. In both cases, the insurance company will need your policy numbers and, possibly, a certified death certificate. If you were receiving health coverage under your spouse's employer plan, you may be able to continue on the group plan for 36 months through COBRA coverage. For those on Medicare, you will need to contact Medicare to remove your spouse as an insured. And be sure to contact any insurance companies through which you have Medicare supplemental coverage.

Homeowner's insurance

Your home insurance policy will need to be reviewed if you are staying in the current residence. You will need to contact the insurance company to remove the deceased as an insured and to make sure that you are listed as the insured. Typically you have 30 days to notify the insurance company. The insurance company will most likely need a certified copy of the death certificate. You should also review any personal property listed on the policy.

Life insurance

File a claim for any policy under which the deceased spouse was insured, including individual life insurance policies, group life insurance policies (contact the employer as mentioned earlier), association life insurance policies, and any death benefits paid from a credit card. To collect the death benefit, you will need to file a claim form, which you can request from the insurance company. When you file a claim, you will need a certified copy of the death certificate. Be sure to read the fine print carefully on the life insurance claim form.

If you are maintaining a life insurance policy, including any group (employer) life insurance policies, be sure to change the beneficiaries.

Long-term care insurance

If your spouse or domestic partner had a long-term care insurance policy, be sure to terminate the policy and request a pro rata refund of any unearned premiums. If you have a marital (or domestic partner) discount, it will not be removed.

YOUR INSURANCE NEEDS FOR EACH LIFE STAGE

Life stage	Type of insurance						
	Auto (if you have a car)	Disability (if earning an income)	Health	Homeowner's/renter's (if you own a home or rent)	Life (if someone is financially dependent on you)	Long-term care	Annuities
College years	Yes	Yes	Yes	Yes	Probably no	No	No
Single years	Yes	Yes	Yes	Yes	Probably no	No	No
Employed	Yes	Yes (may need supplemental even if provided by employer)	Yes (if not provided by employer)	Maybe	Maybe	Yes (if age 50+)	No
Business owner or self-employed	Yes	Yes	Yes (if not covered through spouse)	Yes	Maybe	Yes (if age 50+)	No
Married or domestic partners	Yes	Yes	Yes (if not provided by an employer)	Yes	Probably yes	Yes (if age 50+)	No
Parent of a minor	Yes	Yes	Yes	Yes	Yes	Yes (if age 50+)	No
Divorce and dissolutions	Yes	Yes	Yes	Yes	Probably no	Yes (if age 50+)	No
Retirement (and senior years)	Yes	No	Yes (age 65—Medicare)	Yes (unless living in a facility/community)	Most likely not	Yes (if age 50+)	Maybe

PART II

Your Insurance Portfolio:
Building a Strong Team

"There is an old saying about the strength of the wolf is the pack, and I think there is a lot of truth to that. On a football team, it's not the strength of the individual players, but it is the strength of the unit and how they all function together."
—BILL BELICHICK

CHAPTER 3

Auto Insurance: Selecting Your Running Back

"Success isn't owned. It's leased.
Rent is due every day."
—J. J. WATT

So far, you've learned the rules of the game. Now we're going to break this down and talk about your key players. J. J. Watt is the best defensive player in the NFL and, if he plays long enough and at this same level, will be known as one of the best of all time. J. J. has appeared in Pro Bowls four out of his first five full NFL seasons. What J. J. recognizes is that even though he's already excelling, he has to keep working hard.

If you're reading this book, you most likely already have an auto insurance policy. Since you are most likely required to have auto insurance, you need to review your auto insurance policy to ensure that it excels at providing you the coverage you need at the lowest premium.

WHY DO I NEED AUTO INSURANCE?

Like the running back who looks out for the quarterback and the other offensive members of his team, auto insurance provides protection for you and others from losses involving your car.

At some point in your life, you will be involved with an event resulting in an auto claim. The average driver has a comprehensive or collision claim approximately once every eleven years. Every state requires that you carry minimum levels of auto insurance coverage, or the equivalent in financial responsibility waivers in New Hampshire, to ensure that you can cover the cost of damages to people or property in the event of a car accident.

Auto insurance requirements vary from state to state, so be sure to check with your state insurance regulator to learn more about requirements and low-cost auto insurance programs. A table with current requirements can be found on my website.

WHAT DOES AUTO INSURANCE COVER?

Auto insurance provides property, liability, and medical coverage. There are generally six different kinds of coverage. Most states require you to buy some but not all of these coverages. If you're financing a car, your lender may also have requirements. To learn the specific requirements in your state, visit http://www.dmv.org.

Required coverage in nearly every state

Bodily injury liability

Bodily injury liability insurance covers you for injuries that you, as the designated driver or policyholder, cause to someone else. You and the family member listed on the policy are also covered when driving someone else's car (with their permission). This is usually described in three numbers, which refer to limits for the different types of liability coverage. These coverage limits are the most your insurance policy will pay for (1) injuries to any one person, (2) all persons injured in an accident, and (3) property damage.

Property damage liability

This coverage pays for damages you cause to someone else's car or to objects and structures your car hits.

Coverage that may be required in your state

Uninsured and underinsured motorist coverage

Uninsured motorist coverage reimburses you if an uninsured or a hit-and-run driver hits you. Underinsured motorist coverage pays when an at-fault driver doesn't have enough insurance to fully pay for your loss.

Medical payments or personal injury protection (PIP)

PIP insurance provides coverage for the treatment of injuries to the driver and passengers of the insured's (policyholder's) car. Coverage can include medical payments, lost wages, and the cost of replacing services normally provided by the injured person. It may even cover funeral costs.

Coverage required by a lender

While the following coverage is typically required when receiving an auto loan, it is also good coverage for most drivers.

Collision

This coverage pays for damage to your car from a collision with another car, an object or pothole, or from flipping over.

Comprehensive

This coverage reimburses you for damage to your car that's not caused by a collision. This includes theft, hail, windstorm, flood, fire, and hitting animals. Comprehensive coverage will also reimburse you if your windshield is pitted, cracked, or damaged. Some companies won't charge you a deductible for windshield repairs.

No-fault

If you live in a no-fault state, your own insurance company pays for injuries to you and your passengers, regardless of who's at fault. Most no-fault states also let you sue the at-fault driver if you have serious injuries. However, you must still file a claim with the at-fault driver's insurance company to be paid for damage to your vehicle.

Do I need to carry proof of insurance?

States may also require motorists to have physical proof of valid insurance, which is usually a card issued by the insurer. They may also require motorists to provide evidence of insurance in certain situations, including carrying it all at times in their vehicle to present if pulled over by the police, if involved in an accident, or when registering a car. Penalties for driving without mandatory insurance include fines, which can be as high as $5,000 for a subsequent offense, to license or registration suspension or revocation. Some states can impose jail time, confiscate license plates, and impound vehicles.

WHAT SHOULD I LOOK FOR WHEN PURCHASING AUTO INSURANCE?

Go beyond the basics and decide if the minimum coverage required by your state (and lender) meets your needs. Remember these requirements are your floor. Your ceiling could be much higher.

TIP

When purchasing auto insurance, check to see if your state offers no-fault insurance. In no-fault states, each driver pays for their own injuries with their own auto insurance policy, regardless of who is at fault. This applies only to bodily injury.

What are some additional coverages that I can add to an auto insurance policy?

Auto repair insurance

Auto repair insurance covers the natural wear and tear on a vehicle, independent of damages related to a car accident. It does not provide coverage for a vehicle when it is damaged in a collision, during a natural disaster, or at the hands of vandals.

Rental car reimbursement

If you are not at fault, a rental car is normally covered by the at-fault driver's insurance while your vehicle is being repaired. If you were at fault or you have damage caused by a weather event, you would have coverage for all or part of the cost of a rented care while your own vehicle is in the shop being repaired as part of a covered claim.

Roadside service

Roadside service covers towing and other standard roadside assistance programs. Be sure to read through the details and compare with a stand-alone service, such as AAA, on what is covered and what is not. You may also have access to a roadside service through your automobile manufacturer if you are purchasing a new car.

Vanishing deductible

Sometimes referred to as a *disappearing deductible*, a vanishing deductible decreases by a certain amount every year that you don't have a claim. Usually, the cost is not worth it.

Accident forgiveness

With accident forgiveness, the first time you make a claim, your rates won't increase.

New car replacement

New car replacement is also known as *GAP* (*Guaranteed Asset Protection*) insurance. The premium through a dealership is much more expensive than through an auto insurance company, and the dealership may add this to their high-pressure list. Don't fall for it. This covers the difference between the current value and the price of a new car. Be sure to review all restrictions.

How much coverage should I purchase?

Consider your own personal situation, and don't be guided by state insurance coverage minimums. Following are some guidelines.

Bodily injury liability

The minimum you should purchase is the standard 100/300/100 coverage. What this means is that you get coverage up to $100,000 per person per bodily injury, including death, that you cause to others; $300,000 in bodily injury per accident; and $100,000 in property damage. If you have substantial assets, consider increasing this to cover to 250/500 as protection against a personal lawsuit.

Collision

Your maximum collision coverage is usually the book value of your car as defined by your insurance company. Therefore, different insurance companies may have slightly different valuations of the same car. If the annual premium for the collision insurance is equal to or exceeds 10 percent of your car's cash value, you should consider terminating it.

Comprehensive

Your maximum coverage is usually the book value of your car as defined by your insurance company. Again, different insurance companies may have different valuations. Like collision insurance, if the annual premium for the comprehensive insurance is equal to or exceeds 10 percent of your car's cash value, you should consider terminating it.

Medical payments or personal injury protection (PIP)

PIP coverage benefits vary by state. Consider carrying as much as you can afford, to protect yourself from unforeseen injuries resulting from auto accidents.

Uninsured and underinsured motorist

For uninsured or underinsured motorist insurance, purchase the same coverage limits as those on your own liability coverage (they typically cannot exceed the amount of liability coverage). Consider that the average cost of damage in a car accident is $7,500 (not including any medical bills). This can be purchased in two parts: motorist bodily injury related coverage, which protects you on medically related expenses, and property damage coverage for your car. You should purchase both to be fully protected.

TIP

Do you let other people drive your car? In most states, the auto insurance policy on the car at fault is considered the vehicle's primary coverage—regardless of who is operating the car. This means that your insurance is responsible for any damages, although the driver's insurance may cover any costs over your coverage. Insurance regulations vary from state to state, so be sure to check on how this works in your state if you are planning to let someone else drive your car.

HOW DO I MAXIMIZE THE VALUE OF MY AUTO INSURANCE?

Each insurance company uses its own method to calculate premiums, which vary on a number of key factors, including gender, age, marital status, occupation, zip code, driving record, credit history, insurance score, type of car, insurance history, mileage, and claims history. For more details on these factors, visit my website.

To optimize your premium, be sure to review with your agent or company exactly what discounts your company offers. Here is a list of my top ten tips for keeping your insurance costs low:

- Compare policies. You should obtain three to four quotes from different companies, ensuring that they are for the same coverage limits and riders.
- Choose the right deductible. The higher your deductible (the amount you pay out of pocket), the lower your premium.
- Bundle policies. You may receive a discount for obtaining multiple policies from one insurance company (from 5 to 20 percent).
- Pay the premium annually. Insurance companies have "convenience" fees for non-annual premium payments. You can save up to 10 percent by paying annually.
- Report low mileage: Usually, if you drive less than 7,500 miles per year, you can apply for this discount, which will require you to document your mileage at certain periods.
- Ask about loyalty discounts. You may get a discount for staying with the same insurance company, although a few insurance companies will actually increase your premium after a certain number of years.
- Buy an older car. Because the value is less, the cost to insure will be less.
- Report your safety devices. Having airbags, motorized seat belts, antilock brakes, and other factory-installed safety features, as well as antitheft devices, can result in discounts up to 25 percent.
- Ask about group discounts. Professional associations, worker's unions, large employers, and membership organizations can qualify for savings.
- Go claim free. You may be eligible for a no-claim bonus if you have no claims and no moving violations in the policy year.

HOW AND WHEN SHOULD I
REVIEW MY COVERAGE?

Every good general manager checks their roster frequently to ensure that their team is optimized with the best players where they feel they can get an edge. It's important to do a rate check every two or three years, based on all the various factors mentioned in this chapter. Insurance companies will vary in terms of their competitiveness on price and benefits. The only way to know for sure if your coverage is optimized is to review your coverage.

TIP

Review any renewal notice for premium increases or changes in your policy coverage. Make sure that all of your information is accurate and up to date.

The following are specific events that require an immediate review of your auto insurance as they will impact your premium:

- You received a premium increase.
- You sold or otherwise disposed of an existing car or are no longer driving your car.
- You obtained a new car.
- You've moved to a new state or even a new zip code.
- You changed how many miles you drive annually (e.g., a change in commute or retirement).
- You added or removed a driver.
- Your car is paid off and old enough that you would not repair it if it were damaged (consider dropping collision or comprehensive coverage).
- You have a positive increase in your credit.

- You change your potential liability (e.g., driving in a car pool or participating in a ridesharing service).

Pull out your policy or the declarations pages, along with records of any at-fault claims and moving violations.

Review the earlier part of this section to familiarize yourself with your coverage needs to see if you have the right amount of coverage for your current needs. Do you need to increase coverage or can you drop certain coverage?

Notate the pricing factors and which discounts you might qualify for (such as mileage-based pricing may not have been available when you purchased your policy).

Review your company's financial strength ratings and financials.

Review the deductible on your policy to see if it's still optimal.

Obtain three to four new quotes and compare on an apples-to-apples basis with your current coverage (same coverage limits and riders).

TIP

In a number of states, insurance companies must file any rate increases with the resident's state insurance department subject to their approval. The insurance companies must justify that the rate increase is necessary. However, this varies by state insurance department.

What should I do if my auto insurance policy is canceled or not renewed?

Should this happen, you should both seek to reinstate your policy and seek out replacement quotes. Be sure to find out the exact reason your policy was canceled, because this may help you when you are seeking out alternative coverage. If you are negotiating reinstate-ment, the insurer may reconsider with changes to your policy, such as increasing the deductible or removing coverages; however, be sure not to give up something you need. Some reasons for cancellation are out of your control.

If the company is going out of business or discontinuing auto cov-erage, you will need a new company. These are both considered *nonre-newals* and will not impact your premiums as long as there is no gap in coverage, so start your shopping as soon as you receive notice. Be sure to notify your state's DMV of your new insurance carrier (if applicable in your state).

Having a cancellation for the following reasons will likely cause higher premiums with other insurance companies and may impact your ability to get insurance at all.

- Nonpayment of premium. You may be able to apply for reinstatement.
- Driver's license revocation or suspension. You may need an SR-22 certificate.
- Fraud or misrepresentation on an application
- Claim frequency or severity

For this last example, you may be able to appeal the company's decision. Speak with your agent, or if you are directly insured, with the company. You should also start getting other quotes immediately while being up-front with the other providers; you should explain your claims history before getting a quote.

If you commit fraud, you may be subject to criminal prosecution. Honesty is always the best policy. Insurance companies spend a lot of time and money on fighting fraud, so although you may get away with it for a while, it is unlikely to end well for you.

> **TIP**
>
> It is important to apply for reinstatement if your insurance company cancels your policy. This will help you get lower premiums if your policy is reinstated. The reason for the cancellation will be important. On later applications, you will need to carefully answer the question of whether you have ever had a policy nonrenewed or canceled to ensure that you address it accurately and completely. This question varies in wording from company to company. Be sure to provide the insurance company with full details.

WHAT SHOULD I KNOW ABOUT FILING A CLAIM?

There are approximately 10 million car crashes in the United States every year, according to the National Safety Council. Being in a car crash can be disorienting, even if it's just a fender bender.

These are the most important steps to take following a car crash; they will help you during the claims process. Please visit my website for more tips.

- Contact the police (if you haven't already contacted 911) to file an accident report. However, be advised that in a growing number of jurisdictions, police do not come out for noninjury accidents.
- Locate witnesses and get contact information for them, whether or not the police are coming. This can be helpful for any insurance claims.
- Do not imply in any way that you might be at fault. Stick to the facts. If you're moving and the other driver hits you, you may still have a degree of fault, which the insurance companies will figure out. If you admit fault, your insurance company will have to pick up 100 percent of the claim.
- Exchange information. You must always exchange information with the other driver, even if there does not appear to be any

damage. Write down the names of all drivers involved in the accident; the address and phone number of all drivers involved; the year, make, model, and license plate numbers of the cars involved in the accident; and insurance policy numbers. Take a photo of the other driver's license, insurance card, and license plate.

- Document the damage. Take photos showing the damage as well as longer-range photos showing the surroundings and location, such as a street sign or business signage. Take the photos of the damage from multiple angles. Include photos of all four sides of the vehicles, even if they're not damaged. Be sure to take photos before moving any of the vehicles.

- Write down as many details as you can, as soon as you can, such as time, date, weather, traffic conditions, and a full description of the accident. Draw a diagram showing the streets and the direction you were traveling, and describe any injuries, damage, and the details of any police or emergency involvement.

- Call your insurance company as soon as possible. Most companies will also allow you to open a claim inside their mobile app or online. This allows you to provide the information immediately and while details are still fresh in your mind.

What happens after I file a claim?

The insurance company will assign an adjuster to contact both parties and their statements about what happened. The insurance company will then assess the information and determine who is at fault.

TIP

Wait for approval from the insurance company prior to doing any repair work (or having a medical procedure); otherwise, you may be responsible for those costs.

If you are at fault, the insurance company will start the process of getting the other party's vehicle repaired.

If the other driver is at fault, the other driver's insurance company will begin the repair process for you. If they don't have insurance, this is why you will be happy you have uninsured/underinsured motorist coverage.

If fault is disputed, there will be a claim investigation where you are represented by your insurer, and both insurance companies will come to a determination. In some states, each driver can be found partially responsible.

TIP

Keep in mind that informing your insurer about an incident is not the same as filing a claim. Remember that sometimes a claim isn't worth filing—usually when it's not much more than your deductible. Many insurance companies have requirements in their contracts that policy owners must let them know about any event that might lead to a claim.

What happens if I get in an accident when I'm in a different state?

If you get into an accident in another state that has higher minimum limits than your state of residence, insurance companies will typically increase your coverage to meet those higher limits through a broadening clause. If you are in a no-fault state that requires personal injury protection (PIP), your insurance company will also typically extend coverage to pay for any injuries you sustain.

Do I need an attorney?

You would usually involve an attorney when someone is injured, especially if they were badly injured. It's advisable for both drivers to have a lawyer represent their interests properly. You may wish to engage an attorney for these other reasons:

- There was a fatality and you were at fault.
- You're having trouble with your insurance company.
- The incident took place in a construction zone.
- The police report is inaccurate or lists you as at fault when you weren't.
- You have questions or confusion about anything beyond the basics.
- If the other party obtains counsel (let lawyers deal with lawyers).

Determining who's at fault is not an exact science. Each state has its own regulations, and each insurance company has their own way of handling claims. If you live in a no-fault state, the *no-fault* status refers only to injuries; it does not include property damage.

What should I look out for during the repairs?

Your insurance company may urge you to use auto repair shops in a direct-repair program (DRP) or may use cheaper replacement parts, rather than the original equipment manufacturer (OEM) parts. Consumer Reports and others have reported that, during testing, some non-OEM parts fit poorly, are more prone to rust and corrosion, and fail to meet federal safety standards. These non-OEM parts are often cheaper, which is why the insurance companies prefer them. Some states give you the right to choose the repair shop and replacement parts for your car. Check with your state insurance department to see what rights you have.

TIP

Don't file small claims. For example, if you have repairs that will cost $600 and a deductible of $500, there is no reason to file a claim for $100 that could end up costing you more in additional premiums and could keep you from a no-claim bonus (assuming your company has one).

Do I need to worry about fraud?

Below are some of the different types of insurance scams out there. Avoid being a victim or perpetrator of fraud at all costs.

Agent fraud

Make sure that you receive a policy and that it is from the company. Verify that it's a real company through your state insurance department. Contact the insurance company to verify that the coverage in force is the same as what you applied for. Also, be sure that the agent has not added extra coverage onto your policy; this is called *sliding*.

Chipped windshield scam

You may receive an offer to fix your chipped windshield with no out-of-pocket expense, and the entity fixing the windshield may file a claim for a higher amount, which causes an increase in your premiums at renewal.

Fake injury claims

Fake injury claims occur when there's a minor fender bender. Everything seems to be okay, but a few days later, the other driver or their passenger claims whiplash or other injuries. That's why it's recommended to file a policy report if possible and to immediately start the insurance claims process with full documentation.

Fraudulent car repairs

A mechanic may install substandard parts. The best remedy is to take your car to a reputable mechanic. Check with the Better Business Bureau or consult your insurance company's recommended repair shops list.

Staged accidents

Staged accidents can be very elaborate and can include a whole team of fake witnesses, doctors, and legal advisors who may provide false or misleading testimony or advice. Be aware that they will often have "helpers" who may try to get your personal information or be overeager to help. This can make it challenging for you to prove what really happened. Insurance companies are very aware of the most common types of staged accidents and can help determine if an accident was staged. This is another good reason to contact your insurance company about every accident and provide full and complete information even if you do not plan on filing a claim. An insurance company has the resources and knowledge to help you not be a victim.

WHAT ARE SOME OTHER TYPES OF AUTO INSURANCE I SHOULD KNOW ABOUT?

Business auto insurance

Insurers may deny claims for damage or injuries to your private vehicle when it is used for business. State laws and insurance company standards will vary; however, if you fall into any of the following situations, you should consider adding business auto insurance:

- Using your car regularly for business
- Registering your car in the name of your business
- Using your car to regularly transport tools or equipment to job sites
- Pulling a trailer with equipment or merchandise

Commercial insurance comes with higher coverage limits and adds an additional layer of protection for both your personal and your business assets.

Car sharing

You cannot currently obtain insurance for car sharing. If you decide to rent out your car to someone else, your policy will be cancelled immediately if the insurance company finds out. Insurance companies are not able to underwrite potential drivers and will therefore not cover it. Also, consider that if your renter causes an at-fault accident, you will almost certainly be named in the lawsuit as the owner of the car, and if the renter is injured, they can bring a liability claim against you for a myriad of reasons such as bad tires or bad brakes.

Company car

Your company will almost certainly have full auto insurance coverage. There are two areas that may not be covered, however. The first is injuries you cause to coworkers riding with you; an extended, nonowner automobile coverage endorsement can be added to your personal auto insurance policy to cover you in this case. The second is, unless your personal auto insurance covers you driving any car, your employer can add a broad drive-other-cars coverage endorsement to the business policy. If the employer does not wish to do so, you can purchase a named nonowner auto insurance policy.

Family (or other personal car) available for regular use

Be sure that any driver is listed on the policy. If a family member is no longer driving, be sure to transfer the title as well to ensure that all drivers are properly covered.

Hourly rentals

You will need to inquire about what type of coverage is provided by the rental service that you use. For example, Zipcar provides primary liability coverage of $300,000, along with primary collision and comprehensive coverage with deductibles. If you have personal auto insurance coverage, it would potentially supplement the Zipcar coverage (read your policy). And if you do not have a personal policy and would like additional coverage, you can purchase a named nonowner personal auto insurance policy.

Rental car coverage

Rental coverage is one of the most confusing and misunderstood areas of auto insurance. Any liability, medical, and uninsured or underinsured motorist coverage may transfer to a rental car in the United States or Canada. Your collision and comprehensive coverage will transfer and will cover the rental car, but potentially only partially. If you are renting a car, look at your policy. There is no transfer in other countries.

It's important to get proof of coverage for a rental car in writing from your agent or insurance company. Rental car companies do offer collision damage waiver (CDW) that will cover all your renter obligations; however, there are still coverage gaps. You have no coverage if you've had a single drink, if you drive carelessly, if you have an unlisted driver who causes an accident, or if you drive on an unpaved road. The CDW is recommended if your auto policy does not transfer to rental cars or if you are renting outside the US or Canada. You may also have CDW through one of your credit cards.

If you have a personal umbrella liability policy, be sure to read it to see if it transfers abroad, as you may also need the liability insurance offered by the rental car company. It's recommended that you take photos of the vehicle before you leave the rental lot, after any accident, and upon returning it, and keep those for your records.

Ridesharing services

Ridesharing services, such as Uber and Lyft, also known as *transportation network companies* (TNCs), contract with drivers to use their own car to provide rides for a fee. Personal, traditional car insurance excludes all coverage while you have a passenger and are looking for passengers. This exclusion applies to liability, uninsured/underinsured motorist, and collision coverage. Please note that a personal umbrella policy would also not cover you.

The TNCs usually provide insurance coverage for themselves and for drivers for $1 million in liability coverage when you have a passenger in your car. Check with your TNC to see what they provide.

There is no coverage while you are waiting for a passenger. A couple of states have passed laws to require TNCs to provide coverage during this period; however, it is minimal. A few companies have started to offer coverage for this gap, and if you are a TNC driver, I strongly recommend that you obtain this coverage.

If you are the passenger, be sure to check what coverage the TNC company has; if you are injured while riding, you would report a claim to the TNC's insurer.

Motorcycle insurance

Depending on your perspective, riding a motorcycle is a risky proposition. There is a higher rate of accidents for motorcycles than for cars. The main risks are damaging your motorcycle, someone else's property, and yourself, a passenger, or another person. Motorcycle insurance, for the most part, functions like auto insurance.

A majority of states require a minimum amount of motorcycle insurance, but Florida and Washington do not currently require it. Florida does require proof of financial responsibility if you choose to forgo motorcycle insurance. Each state has its own minimum requirements for bodily injury and property damage liability—the amount a policyholder's motorcycle insurance company will cover. Visit my website for more information.

TIP

Insurance coverage may also be required for mopeds, scooters, dirt bikes, and trikes, so be sure to check with your state's motor vehicle department on insurance requirements.

CHAPTER 4

Disability Insurance: Selecting Your Wide Receiver

"Do you know what my favorite part of the game is?
The opportunity to play."
—MIKE SINGLETARY

ootball players realize that every day they can play is a good day—
and with good reason: Football players are at a greater risk of
injury than anyone. It is rare to have an NFL game where a player
does not incur an injury that keeps them from playing the next week
or longer. In a survey conducted of ex-NFL players, the former players
stated they were still affected by their injuries: knees (70 percent), lower
back (67 percent), shoulders (65 percent), neck (56 percent), and head
(49 percent).

It is common practice for NFL players to carry disability insurance
policies paid for either by their team or personally. The NFL does provide a minimal policy with current coverage limits of $180,000, which is
not much, considering the high odds of getting injured and sustaining
long-term damage.

The good news is that your odds of filing for disability are significantly less than those of someone playing in the NFL. However, you still
need to be prepared, in case you do sustain an injury that could reduce
or sever your income.

DO I NEED DISABILITY INSURANCE?

Everyone is at risk of becoming disabled. Many of us tend to think of becoming disabled as something that happens to other people, particularly to those with physically demanding jobs. But only about 10 percent of all disabling injuries happen on the job. If you are young and fit, you might believe your chances of becoming disabled are less than an older person's; but statistics show that isn't the case, because you have more years during which you might become disabled. Consider the following table:

YOUR CHANCE OF BECOMING DISABLED FOR MORE THAN 90 DAYS BEFORE THE AGE OF 65

Age	Percentage of people disabled	Odds of becoming disabled
25	52%	1 out of 2
30	51%	1 out of 2
35	48%	4 out of 9
40	45%	4 out of 9
45	40%	2 out of 5
50	34%	1 out of 3
55	16%	1 out of 6

Source: 1985 Commissioner's Disability Table

Now, if you're older, this table might make you think the risks associated with becoming disabled are less than they are for a younger person. But again, that isn't the case. The problem older people face is that their disabilities tend to last much longer, as you can see in the following table. And, given the fact that the age for the onset of receiving Social Security benefits has continued to rise over the years, depending on that government resource is dangerous. Although the table only goes up to age 55, the retirement age for Social Security purposes will soon reach 70 years of age.

**THE OLDER YOU GET THE HIGHER YOUR CHANCES OF
BEING DISABLED FOR LONGER PERIODS OF TIME**

Age	Average length of your disability (in months)	Your chance (percentage) of disability lasting five years or more
20–24	69	30
25–29	74	32
30–34	78	35
35–39	82	38
40–44	85	40
45–49	86	43
50–54	86	45
55+	84	46

Source: The Council on Disability Awareness

To help you understand the importance of protecting your income, you can calculate your potential earnings, then, using the age and income closest to yours, find your potential earnings in the table below. You'll soon see that good health is priceless.

**POTENTIAL EARNINGS TO AGE 65 IN DOLLARS
(WITH FIVE-PERCENT ANNUAL SALARY INCREASES)**

| Age | Current annual income | | | | | |
	$25,000	$50,000	$75,000	$100,000	$150,000	$200,000
30	$2,258,000	$4,516,000	$6,774,000	$9,032,000	$13,548,000	$18,064,000
35	$1,661,000	$3,322,000	$4,983,000	$6,644,000	$9,966,000	$13,288,000
40	$1,193,00	$2,386,000	$3,580,000	$4,773,000	$7,159,000	$9,545,000
45	$827,000	$1,653,000	$2,480,000	$3,307,000	$4,960,000	$6,613,000
50	$539,000	$629,000	$1,618,000	$2,158,000	$3,237,000	$4,316,000
55	$314,000	$629,000	$943,000	$1,58,000	$1,887,000	$2,516,000
60	$138,000	$276,000	$414,000	$553,000	$829,000	$1,105,000

How do I determine how much income protection I actually need?

Every advisor, financial columnist, and relative has a formula they think is best for determining how much long-term disability insurance you need. Some of these formulas are simple, whereas others look like something only a Wall Street numbers whiz could cook up. Don't let complexity overwhelm or discourage you. If your needs are more complex, a qualified disability insurance agent or financial advisor can help you determine the right amount for you. For most people, however, the simplest method is the best. You'll need to replace enough of your income to cover your monthly expenses, with additional coverage to supplement retirement savings (remember to subtract any income that will continue if you are disabled). Visit my website to download a detailed worksheet to help you figure out how much disability insurance you need.

WHAT SHOULD I LOOK FOR IN DISABILITY INSURANCE?

If you are like some people, you may look at the gap between your monthly expenses and income you could rely on in the event of total disability and not be too concerned. You might believe that if you did become disabled, resources such as Social Security, worker's compensation, or group benefits through your job would provide enough protection. Before jumping to that conclusion, however, you should understand the realities of the resources that may—or may not—be available to you.

What kind of disability insurance do I get through my employer?

Employers will typically provide short-term disability benefits in the form of paid sick leave, short-term disability insurance, or both. Coverage can range from a few days to as long as a year, depending on your company's benefits and your length of employment. Short-term disability insurance benefits are typically paid when you are unable to perform the duties of your occupation (this is a more liberal definition of disability than for the Social Security program). Short-term disability insurance benefits are taxable (for the employee) when the employer pays the premium, which is generally the case.

A group long-term disability plan policy offered by your employer will guarantee that you have coverage, which means no underwriting application process is involved. A typical policy through your employer replaces at least half of your salary up to a specific maximum benefit, such as $5,000 or $10,000 per month. Just like the short-term equivalent, long-term disability insurance benefits are taxable to the employee when the employer pays the premium, and the amount of the benefit is offset (i.e., reduced) by the amount of benefits that the insured receives from Social Security or workers' compensation. Some employers offer voluntary long-term disability insurance, where employees may choose to participate and pay their own premiums through payroll deduction. In some cases, the voluntary long-term disability insurance coverage is in lieu of coverage purchased by the employer. More frequently, voluntary long-term disability insurance coverage allows the employee to supplement the long-term disability insurance coverage provided by the employer.

Employer-paid coverage is usually not portable. In other words, if you leave the employer, your coverage is discontinued.

A policy offered by an association or other organization will likely require an application and an underwriting process, although coverage for members of the group is sometimes guaranteed.

Should I be covered beyond what my employer offers?

You can purchase individual disability income insurance from a company on your own that you can customize to meet your needs. Customizing the parameters on your policy will make a difference in the premiums (and benefits). Two factors are especially important here: first, to determine what you most want in a policy and the premium that you can afford and will want to continue to pay each year; and second, to use those parameters to guide your decisions.

If your salary is your sole source of income, it may be important to get the maximum amount of coverage you can afford. If you have passive income (such as from rental properties) that you could count on even if you were disabled, getting maximum coverage may be less important. Benefit amounts can vary from company to company, and the benefit can either be calculated as a percentage of your regular income (typical on a group policy) or be a flat amount (typical on an individual policy). Individual policies will often offer a benefit of approximately 65 percent of your after-tax earnings.

If you are like most people, you view your chances of becoming disabled as slim. You may not receive Social Security benefits because they are difficult to qualify for and are limited. You may not qualify for the programs offered in your state, and you may not have protection through your employer or another organization. In fact, if you are like most people, when you combine your coverage need with an evaluation of possible coverage, you may conclude that having your own income protection in place may be a necessity.

Individual disability insurance policies can also be used to supplement group long-term disability coverage. Unlike group benefits, individual policy benefits are typically not subject to income tax, because the premiums are paid with after-tax dollars. A few employers do offer the option to have your premiums paid after taxes, in which case the benefits received are not subject to income tax.

In addition, individual disability policies typically offer more coverage, because they will insure all earned income (including commissions and bonuses), whereas group long-term disability insurance plans do not usually cover commissions and bonuses and can have a maximum benefit. Individual policies also offer greater flexibility in terms of elimination period, benefit period, and optional riders in the design of the policy. Even if you have the option to purchase disability coverage through your employer (where you pay the premiums), an individual policy will generally be less expensive over the long term than a group policy if you are in good health.

To fully understand your need for an individual disability insurance policy and to determine if you have a coverage gap, download the disability insurance protection and coverage gap worksheet on my website.

How do I determine the differences in core components of a disability insurance policy?

Every disability insurance policy has certain core definitions and parameters that can differ from company to company. These include the amount of the benefit, how *disability* is defined, how *sickness* is defined, the benefit period, and the elimination period.

How is *disability* defined?

The definition of *disability* is the most important part of the policy, because everything else stems from it. Some policies pay benefits only if you are unable to perform the duties of any occupation for which you are reasonably qualified by training, experience, and education. A typical definition may read, "You are unable to perform with reasonable continuity the substantial and material acts necessary to perform your regular occupation in the usual and customary way." Other policies pay benefits if you are unable to perform the major duties of your own occupation. This feature used to be common. However, depending on the definition in current contracts, it's not always necessary.

What is presumptive disability?

All policies include a statement of presumptive disability—a level of disability that automatically qualifies you for full benefits for the complete benefit period. It usually involves the loss of one or more of the following:

- Sight in both eyes (below 20/200)
- Speech
- Hearing in both ears (not restorable with the use of a hearing aid)
- The use of one hand or one foot

If you suffer from these types of disabilities, you aren't required to prove the level of your disability. The insurance company presumes you will not recover.

How is "sickness" defined?

Sickness is typically defined by when an illness began. It is better if the wording in the policy is *when it first manifests* rather than *when first contracted*. The difference between the two is significant, especially, for example, if the disability is caused by cancer. Under the first definition, even if cancer existed when the policy was issued but it had not yet appeared or would not have caused a prudent person to seek medical attention, it would be covered. Under the second definition, it would not be covered if it could be proven to have existed prior to the effective date of the policy. This difference may not be as crucial if you are young and in good health. The chances of your having a serious illness at the time you buy a policy are not as great when you are younger or in good health as when you are older or have some health concerns.

Is the policy guaranteed renewable or noncancelable?

Most disability policies are either guaranteed renewable or noncancelable. Most policies are noncancelable in the base contract, but some insurers offer the option to make them guaranteed renewable.

A guaranteed renewable policy guarantees that the insurer cannot terminate the policy as long as the premiums are paid, and the insured (you) doesn't have to reapply at any point to continue coverage. With a guaranteed renewable policy, premiums cannot be raised based on your circumstances, but they can be increased for an entire class of policyholders. No other aspect of the policy can be changed for the life of the policy.

A noncancelable policy takes guaranteed renewable a step further. It offers the same parameters or protections that guaranteed renewable offers but also specifies that premiums can never be increased. Most disability policies today automatically include this.

A noncancelable policy can be substantially more expensive than a guaranteed renewable policy; when a company offers the option, the premium could be 50 percent greater. You're paying that additional cost to protect yourself against a potential, unknown, and uncertain premium increase. Yet the company may not ever increase the premium. So you need to weigh that protection against the substantial cost increase.

How do I structure my disability insurance coverage?

A disability policy allows plenty of options for customizing your coverage to best fit your needs. Individual policies allow you to pick and choose policy components that impact coverage and premiums. With disability insurance policies, however, there can be big differences from company to company and policy to policy in terms of which policy components are automatically woven into the policy, which are offered as optional riders, and which are not offered at all. Review the following policy riders to determine which configuration riders would be most appropriate for your needs.

Benefit period

When choosing your policy, you can decide what benefit period you want. This means that if you became disabled, you would receive benefits for a certain period or until you reach the specified age. Typically, it's two or five years or until age 65, 67, or 70.

Waiting period

After a qualifying disability, there is a waiting period—also known as an *elimination period*—before you can begin receiving benefits. The shorter the elimination period, the costlier the policy. On a group policy offered by an employer, the elimination period will usually dovetail with the benefit period for the employer's short-term disability program (to eliminate any gap in coverage, although the benefit amounts may differ). Elimination periods can vary from one month to one year, although 90 days is the norm.

Partial disability insurance rider

A partial disability is one that keeps you from doing part of your job or from working full time. A residual or partial disability rider covers you if you go from being totally disabled to being able to return to work part time. With this rider, you would collect a percentage of the total benefit based on your loss of earnings. Some policies require you to be totally disabled for a period of time before the insurance company will pay a residual or partial disability claim.

Future increase (purchase) option

This option allows the policy owner to apply for additional coverage based solely on financial underwriting, without any medical underwriting. This is especially beneficial if you were to develop health issues. This option is usually offered at certain intervals until a specific cut-off age, but keep these three variations of a future increase in mind:

- Optional increase: You may apply once per year for a coverage increase when you experience an increase in earnings.
- Benefit update: This version provides an opportunity to increase coverage at predetermined intervals of time.
- Future purchase option: If you purchase an increased amount of coverage, it will come from a pool you've previously purchased.

Premiums for coverage obtained through this type of option will be based on the company's current premium schedule, the type of policy offered at that time, and your age at the time you apply for the increase. Future increase premiums are not based on the premiums of the original policy. This option is very important because your health is never guaranteed; no medical underwriting ensures that you will be eligible for coverage as long as you qualify financially. It may be especially important for small business owners who are still in the start-up phase and don't have a history of income in the business to prove insurability.

Extended/transition benefit

An extended or transition benefit allows you to be paid as if you were still disabled when you are no longer under a doctor's care (even though you have returned to work full-time), as long as there is more than a

20 percent loss of income. Some companies offer this benefit for different periods of time (e.g., 12 or 24 months), while others offer it for the full benefit period (until age 65).

Recovery benefit

A recovery benefit is a lump sum paid immediately following your recovery from a partial disability. This lump sum amount varies by carrier, but it is usually in the range of three to six times the monthly benefit amount.

Return-to-work or rehabilitation provisions

The insurer will pay for training, modifications to your work environment, or other services that assist you in returning to work if you have this rider.

Lost income provision

This benefit provision makes up for your loss in income if you must take a lower-paying job because of your disability.

Waiting period relapse waiver

With this rider, the waiting period to receive benefits is waived if you go back to work after recovering from a disability and have a relapse within a specified period, such as six months.

Cost-of-living adjustment or inflation benefit

This rider provides for periodic increases in the amount paid. These usually correspond to increases in your cost of living, and they can be based on the consumer price index or a fixed percentage increase. Typically, this benefit commences one year after a claim starts to pay.

Mental health extended coverage

Policies usually pay benefits for a maximum of two years in the case of disabilities resulting from mental health problems or substance abuse. This rider provides coverage for the full benefit period.

Catastrophic disability benefit rider

This rider provides a monthly benefit in addition to your monthly disability benefit (and social insurance supplement, if there is one on the policy) in the event that you become catastrophically disabled solely due to an injury or sickness and lose the ability to perform two or more activities of daily living without assistance, become cognitively impaired, or become presumptively disabled. If any of these things happen, the carrier will presume you are totally disabled for the rest of the benefit period.

Supplemental social insurance rider

This rider pays an extra benefit if you meet the insurance company's definition of total disability but not the criteria for Social Security Disability Insurance (SSDI).

HOW DO I MAXIMIZE THE VALUE OF MY POLICY?

As I mentioned in the last chapter, each insurance company uses its own method to calculate their premiums, which vary on several key factors such as gender, age, health, lifestyle (travel, sports, and activities), and occupation.

The insurance industry breaks occupations into classes based on risk factors. That classification takes into account the daily duties on the job. The better the risk factors for a class, the lower the premium. The occupation doesn't necessarily gauge the risk; rather, it gauges the nature of business. Not all insurers will cover occupational classifications with the greatest risk.

To optimize your premium, be sure to review discounts with your agent or company. I've listed a few below. Be sure to visit my website for more tips.

Select occupation discount

Some occupations qualify for a discount (usually 10 percent) with certain insurance companies, including actuaries, architects, attorneys, certified public accountants, engineers, executives (earning more than $60,000), judges, pharmacists, physicians (including residents), and more.

Choose the mode of premium payment

Insurance companies typically charge more when you pay other than annually. Changing how often you pay your premium could save you money.

Multiple policy discounts

If you are a business owner, for example, and you purchase an individual disability insurance policy and a business overhead expense policy, you may be eligible for a discount.

Multi-life discounts

For employers insuring at least three people, you may be eligible for a discount between 10 and 20 percent.

Purchase insurance through a professional group or association

Groups are usually able to negotiate lower premiums, so you may get a lower rate through a professional association.

IS MY DISABILITY INSURANCE PERFORMING WELL?

Disability insurance doesn't end when you purchase a policy. Policies are living things, and many components can affect their performance. Plus, your needs may change over time. To ensure that you have all of the income protection you need, you must learn to monitor your policy carefully. You can find a worksheet on my website.

One important factor to be aware of is the possibility of future premium increases. A noncancelable rider guarantees stable premiums. On the majority of individual disability insurance policies, this rider is automatically included, so your premium is likely guaranteed. That can assist you in your overall budgeting. However, it may not be included. You must keep that in mind so you can budget for possible increases.

Are there any exclusions on my policy that can be removed?

Often an individual disability insurance policy is issued with exclusions for a certain condition, such as an exclusion for a recent wrist injury. If a condition is excluded, any disability resulting from that injury or illness would not be covered. These exclusions can sometimes be removed after a certain period. Sometimes the company will indicate that period of time when a policy is issued, and other times it needs to be brought to the company's attention for consideration. This is why it is important to monitor your policy and be proactive. An exclusion will be removed only if there has been no recurrence of the original issue. Some exclusions cannot ever be removed.

It's important to note that it will be entirely up to you to pursue changes to your policy or to get an exclusion removed. Even if there is a timeline set for the exclusion, don't assume that your insurance company will automatically remove it. Make a note to contact them at the end of the set period to make sure that the exclusion is removed.

When you contact the company to ask that an exclusion be removed, they may ask you to provide proof that there has been no recurrence of the injury or any ongoing health issues related to the exclusion. Be prepared to provide medical information to back up your request.

What if I have a future purchase option or future increase option?

If you have one of these options on your disability insurance policy, you may have an opportunity to increase your disability insurance coverage without any medical underwriting, regardless of your health. These terms are based on the definitions of the FPO (or FIO) feature of your policy and are usually reserved for policyholders under age 50. The amount available to you is tied to your earnings. Some policies require you to notify the carrier within 90 days of an increase in earnings. Other types of policies will allow you to trigger the FIO on policy anniversary dates only. You should review your policy anytime you have an increase in annual earnings to see if it is an appropriate time to exercise the FPO or FIO.

What happens to my group long-term disability policy if I leave my employer?

If you leave your employer, you will most likely lose your group long-term disability insurance coverage. You may or may not receive notification that coverage is terminated. It is rare for a group long-term disability insurance policy to be portable.

If you are planning on leaving your employer, it's a good idea to obtain individual long-term disability insurance *before* you leave your employer, with the maximum future purchase option rider that you can obtain. This is important because, as we discussed earlier, new businesses can be required to show one to two years of earnings before an insurance company will offer coverage. However, some companies will offer a "starter" disability insurance policy, with a low monthly benefit of $2,000–$2,500.

How do I terminate a disability insurance policy?

An individual disability insurance policy can easily be terminated. All it takes is a phone call to the insurance company. However, keep in mind that once a policy is terminated, it's terminated. Some companies may offer a short reinstatement period, but not all will. Also, newer coverage is most likely going to come at a much higher cost, require underwriting, and have policy definitions that may not be as liberal. If you're terminating due to a cash crunch, you may want to consider making changes to the policy rather than terminating it straight out. Modifications that can reduce your premium include removing riders, reducing coverage, increasing the elimination period, and shortening the benefit period. But keep in mind that these modifications, once made, are permanent and cannot be undone. Your policy may feature the ability to make other modifications, so read it carefully, and review with your agent or the company. They may have other useful suggestions.

Terminating a group disability policy may be a different story. This coverage—at least the base coverage—frequently cannot be terminated, because all employees are insured. If you've purchased supplemental coverage, you may be able to modify it as described above. But you may have to wait until your open enrollment period to make any changes. This is common in group plans.

If you have opted into group coverage through an association, it may be easier to cancel it if you need to.

Should I replace a disability insurance policy?

Replacing a policy is not usually recommended, as older policies are usually lower priced and have more liberal policy definitions. If a new policy does make sense, make sure the new policy is in place prior to terminating your existing policy. But think twice before replacing a disability insurance policy. It usually does not make sense. You can use the disability worksheet from my website to assist you.

HOW DO I FILE A DISABILITY INSURANCE CLAIM?

We all buy income protection policies with the hope that we never have to use them. But many of us will have the misfortune of enduring a disabling event. If that happens, you may be left thinking, *what do I do next?* The most effective thing you can do is to immediately get in contact with the carrier—specifically, their claims department.

Your carrier's claims department will ask you a series of questions to gather enough relevant information in order to trigger the claims process. Sometimes, depending on the carrier, you may have to provide current written notice of the claim and financial documentation, such as a tax return or a pay stub, in order to prove that you are actually enduring a financial burden due to your disability. They may also request verification of such additional information as your occupation, daily duties, and the number of hours you work per week.

The claims department will also request additional information after your initial conversation with them. Of course, they would not begin to pay a claim without the proper notations from your doctor, so plan on alerting your doctor about your disability policy so he or she is prepared to send the required medical information to the carrier. This process verifies your claim and explains that you, in fact, incurred an accident or sickness and that your inability to perform your occupational duties is sufficient to meet the definition contained in the policy you chose to purchase.

Claims through a group disability policy or any other policy that offsets against legislated benefits will also require you to apply for any and all social benefits for which you may be eligible. This may include but is not limited to Social Security DI benefits, workers' compensation, and state DI programs.

Your benefit payments will start coming to you once you've completed all the necessary steps noted here and satisfied your waiting period. Your first check will arrive a month after the *commencement date*, which is the first day immediately following completion of the waiting period. Some carriers may require a continuance of disability form to be completed each month, while others simply require a renewed evaluation from your doctor every few months.

TIP

If you have a policy purchased prior to 2005 or so, insurers included in their policy contracts a stipulation called the "relation to earnings clause" that stated if your income was lower when you become disabled than it was when you purchased the policy, the benefit amount would be lowered. Most policies issued after 2005 do not include this clause.

WHAT ARE THE TAX CONSEQUENCES OF MY CLAIM?

The tax consequences of a claim vary from policy to policy and are usually dependent on who pays the premium. The general rule is that on an individual disability insurance policy where the insured pays the premium, the benefits will not be subject to income tax. On a group disability policy, where an employer pays the premium, the benefits are subject to income tax (except in those situations where the employee elects to pay with after-tax dollars, an option not always offered). Please note that this is not tax advice, and you should consult your tax advisor if you have questions.

ARE THERE OTHER TYPES OF DISABILITY INSURANCE THAT I SHOULD KNOW ABOUT?

What is the Social Security Disability Insurance Program?

The Social Security Administration (SSA) provides long-term disability benefits based on your salary and the number of years you have worked and contributed to the Social Security system. The SSA administers two programs that pay disability benefits: The SSDI program pays benefits to qualified individuals who are under age 65, regardless of their income when they become disabled. The Supplemental Security Income (SSI) program pays benefits only to qualified individuals with limited or no income. Eligible family members may also receive a monthly check equal to as much as 50 percent of your basic benefit. This is in addition to your benefit.

What is workers' compensation insurance?

Workers' compensation is state-mandated indemnity insurance held by employers that covers employees for lost income and medical expenses when injuries or illnesses are work related. Workers' compensation is provided through private insurers. After a short waiting period, it may pay for your medical expenses and a portion of your lost wages. Benefits vary significantly by state and are subject to different maximum and minimum amounts. Typically, these benefits are equal to two-thirds of your pre-disability income. Only 10 percent of disabilities are a result of work-related injuries. Employers can opt out of providing workers' compensation insurance, so check with your human resources department to see if you have this coverage.

What coverage can I get through my state disability program?

Some states offer temporary disability insurance programs that can help you if you become disabled. Not every state does, however, and sometimes they apply only to certain types of workers. Likewise, most of the states that do offer some type of statutory disability insurance offer only temporary or short-term coverage—that is, less than one year.

Do I need short-term disability insurance?

Short-term disability insurance provides coverage for a limited period of time, usually from three to six months, with a short elimination period of usually seven days. This typically covers up to 80 percent of your gross income. Coverage can be expensive if you purchase it as an individual and can be as much as the premium for a long-term disability insurance policy.

How can disability insurance help my business?

The following are the most common types of business-related disability insurance policies:

Business overhead expense (BOE)

BOE protects your regular monthly expenses that will allow your business to operate smoothly if you are unable to pay for your expenses due to a covered disability.

Disability insurance buy–sell agreement (DIBS)

Protects you if your partner becomes disabled. The policy would fund an agreement that mandates the purchase of the disabled partner's portion of the business. The DIBS benefit can be paid to you in an ongoing manner or as a lump sum.

Key person insurance

Key person insurance (sometimes referred to as *key man* insurance) provides coverage for key employees.

CHAPTER 5

Health Insurance: Selecting the Right Quarterback

"I'm not telling you it's going to be easy;
I'm telling you it's going to be worth it."
—RUSSELL WILSON

Russell Wilson came into the NFL as a third-round draft pick and was overlooked due to his height—5'11", which many considered to be too short to be a starting quarterback in the NFL. Wilson has proved that he belongs by taking the Seahawks to the NFL playoffs in all five of his seasons. To achieve this, he had to work hard and to learn. Health insurance is the quarterback of your insurance portfolio, and all of us will need it at some point. It will cover your medical expenses if you are sick or injured, along with providing preventative care. Navigating the world of health insurance is not easy; however, doing so will definitely be worth it for you.

WHY DO I NEED HEALTH INSURANCE?

Under the Patient Protection and Affordable Care Act (also known as the ACA or PPACA or under the nickname *Obamacare*), health care coverage is mandated by law—at least for now. The ACA is currently being threatened with repeal; for current information, visit my website.

Until then, if you do not carry health insurance, you will have to pay a fee unless you qualify for an exemption.

Since you are required by law to carry health insurance and since health care is so important, this really should be an easy decision. If you are young and healthy, you may feel invincible; however, you don't know what you don't know. In other words, you may be fine one day, and the next day, you are diagnosed with a medical issue.

Health insurance is especially important if and when you have a health emergency. The cost for medical services is much higher when paid out of pocket than when paid through health insurance, because insurance companies are able to negotiate for lower-cost services and medications. Medical bills are a leading cause of consumer debt and can lead to bankruptcy and home foreclosure. These costs can add up quickly, and insurance is your most viable protection.

WHAT SHOULD I LOOK FOR IN HEALTH INSURANCE?

Health insurance is a complex topic, and your needs and the type of coverage available will depend on factors such as your age, marital status, and general health. See the "Insurance for All Seasons" chapter for guidance at each major stage of your life. If you are close to or over age 65, there is a section on Medicare at the end of this chapter.

There are two main types of health insurance: private and public. Private health insurance is supplied through your employer or bought from a marketplace. Public health insurance includes plans such as Medicaid, Medicare, and CHIP (the Children's Health Insurance Program).

Which treatments are paid for by insurance?

There are ten categories of services that all health insurance plans cover under the Affordable Care Act, listed as follows:

Ambulatory patient services

Ambulatory—meaning "walking" or "walk-in"—patient services are levels of care that you can receive without being admitted to a hospital. This includes standard doctor's office appointments and in-home health visits.

Emergency services

This includes any care you receive for a potentially debilitating or fatal condition, such as emergency room treatment and ambulance rides.

Hospitalization for surgery, overnight stays, and other conditions

This category includes lab work, medications, and any other treatment received at a hospital or skilled nursing facility.

Pregnancy, maternity, and newborn care

As you might imagine, this includes all prenatal care for expectant mothers, along with labor and delivery.

Mental health and substance use disorder services

This division covers any inpatient or outpatient care necessary to diagnose, monitor, or treat mental illness or addiction. Your plan may limit treatment to a specific number of days, and the services available can vary by state.

Prescription drugs

All health insurance plans come with some level of prescription drug coverage. This helps pay the cost of certain prescription medications, including some over-the-counter drugs that were previously prescription only.

Your insurer will have some restrictions, however. You may be obligated to use generic over name-brand medications, and your plan has a *formulary* (an approved list). The drugs on this list are covered; others are not. This is important because if your medication is not covered, you may end up paying a lot out of pocket. The formulary will include which medications are covered, how much they will cost, and any restrictions. You can access a plan's formulary by visiting the insurance company's website, by reviewing your summary of benefits and coverage (if you have a plan already), by calling the insurance company, or by reviewing any coverage materials.

Insurance companies have grouped medications in their formularies into tiers that are classified according to cost. Different versions of the same medication may fall into different tiers, such as a generic version in tier 1 and the branded version in tier 2. A medication's tier listing is based on its real cost and the insurance company's negotiated price. Tiers will also differ by company.

Insurance companies may also have restrictions on certain medications, including prior authorization requirements, quantity limits, and step therapy (where your company requires you to use at least one less-expensive version before being prescribed a more-expensive version). Insurance companies do change their formularies, so this is something to monitor.

Insurance companies also have a list of excluded drugs, known as *permanent drug exceptions*; however, they do have a process that allows you to receive a prescribed drug that's not normally covered by your health insurance plan. Each insurance company has its own exceptions process. Your doctor must confirm to your insurance company that the drug is appropriate for your medical condition. If your exception is declined, you have the right to appeal the decision and have it reviewed by an independent third party.

Insurance companies will also have rules on which pharmacies you can use—in- and out-of-network (see below)—so be sure to review this as well. If there is not a local in-network pharmacy, you may able to use mail order.

Rehabilitative and habilitative services and devices

This includes treatment and devices that help people gain or recover mental and physical skills after an injury, disability, or onset of a chronic condition, such as physical therapy, occupational therapy, and speech therapy. Some plans may limit the number of sessions per year.

Laboratory services

Any tests necessary to diagnose, monitor, or rule out certain conditions are covered.

Preventive and wellness services

This includes physicals, screenings, immunizations, and other services meant to prevent or detect illness or other conditions, as well as chronic disease management. Most health plans must cover a set of preventive services—like shots and screening tests—at no cost to you, but these services are free only when delivered by a doctor or other provider in your plan's network.

These free services include the following:

- Abdominal aortic aneurysm one-time screening
- Alcohol misuse screening and counseling
- Aspirin use to prevent cardiovascular disease
- Blood pressure screening
- Cholesterol screening
- Colorectal cancer screening
- Depression screening
- Diabetes (type 2) screening
- Diet counseling
- Hepatitis B screening
- Hepatitis C screening
- HIV screening
- Immunization vaccines
- Lung cancer screening
- Obesity screening and counseling
- Sexually transmitted infection prevention counseling
- Syphilis screening
- Tobacco use screening and cessation interventions

Note that some of these screenings may only be for specific age groups. Review your plan or contact your insurer to check which preventive services are free for you.

Women and children have their own set of preventive care benefits. For women, many of the free preventive care benefits are related to pregnancy, breastfeeding, and contraception, as well as gender-specific cancers and sexually transmitted diseases. For children, free preventive care is more focused on developmental disorders and behavioral issues, as well as screenings for common chronic illnesses that can develop in children. You can view these lists at https://www.healthcare.gov/coverage/preventive-care-benefits.

Pediatric services

This includes all care provided to children, including yearly checkups, vaccinations, along with dental and vision coverage.

The specific services offered under these categories may vary from state to state, but these categories represent the minimum that all qualifying health insurance plans are required to cover. All health insurance plans, regardless of whether they are sold on the health insurance exchanges or off-exchange, must cover these ten categories. Plans may choose to cover additional services. State, federal, and private exchanges will show you which exact services each plan covers before you apply.

In addition to the list above, all health insurance plans must also cover birth control and breastfeeding equipment and counseling.

Health insurance plans are not required to cover dental or vision services for adults. To read the full text of the ACA, visit http://www.hhs.gov/healthcare/about-the-law/read-the-law/index.html.

What is a preexisting condition, and why does it matter?

A preexisting condition is any illness, injury, or disability you had before your coverage started. Coverage for preexisting conditions is an important part of the Affordable Care Act. All Marketplace plans must cover treatment for preexisting medical conditions. This means that unlike before the ACA, no insurance plan can reject you, charge you more, or refuse to pay for essential health benefits for these conditions; and once you're enrolled, the plan can't deny you coverage or raise your rates based only on your health. Medicaid and the Children's Health

Insurance Program (CHIP) also can't refuse to cover you or charge you more because of your preexisting condition.

What is a grandfathered plan?

Grandfathered plans don't have to cover preexisting conditions or preventive care. If you have a grandfathered plan and want preexisting conditions covered, you can switch to a Marketplace plan that will cover them during open enrollment or your grandfathered plan year ends, which qualifies you for a special enrollment period.

Why do some plans cover in-network but not out-of-network providers?

A network provider (e.g., a doctor) has agreed to provide benefits or services to the plan's members at prices that the provider and the insurance company have agreed on. The provider generally provides a covered benefit at a lower cost to the plan and the plan's members than if providing the same benefit to someone without insurance or someone with insurance through a plan in which the provider is out of network.

All Marketplace plans are required to have provider networks with enough types of providers to ensure that their plan members can get plan services without unreasonable delay. If you use an out-of-network provider, you may have to pay the full cost of the services you get from that provider, except for emergency services. If you get emergency services from an out-of-network provider, those services are covered by a Marketplace plan as if you used an in-network provider. However, providers may bill you for some additional costs associated with the emergency services you get.

Private health insurance

If you experience a qualifying life event and find yourself shopping for health insurance, don't limit yourself to government-run health insurance exchanges. There are other plans available outside of government exchanges that can also meet your coverage requirements under the Affordable Care Act. To find the plan that best meets your needs and budget, compare the options available through your government exchange with other options available through private online marketplaces like eHealth. Some private marketplaces can also help you apply for government subsidies if you qualify.

What's an on-exchange health insurance marketplace plan?

When the Affordable Care Act was implemented, each state was given the opportunity to create their own health insurance exchange, and if they did not wish to do so, their citizens would participate in the Federal Health Care Exchange at https://www.healthcare.gov. For a current list of states and links to the state marketplaces, see https://www.healthcare.gov/marketplace-in-your-state.

Health insurance plans offered through a state exchange or the federal exchange must cover the ten essential benefits listed earlier, along with any additional services that are mandated by a state. Insurance companies must also offer a plan at every metal tier—as described next.

TIP

Exchange plans are the only private plans for which premium tax credits and cost-sharing reductions (government subsidies for qualifying applicants) are available.

What is a metal tier?

Plans in the Health Insurance Marketplace Metal categories are based on how you and your plan split the costs of your health care—and have nothing to do with quality of care. The four tiers are listed in the following table.

Metal tier	Percentage (%) paid	
	by the insurance company	by you
Bronze	60	40
Silver	70	30
Gold	80	20
Platinum	90	10

"Catastrophic" plans are also available to those under age 30. Depending on how many plans are offered in your area, you may find plans of all or any of these types at each metal level. Silver plans are the only ones that will allow you extra savings—cost-sharing reductions on your deductible, copayment, or coinsurance if you qualify—and more of your routine care is covered.

What should I know about off-exchange private health insurance?

Off-exchange plans are sold directly by a health insurance company, a third-party broker, or a privately run health insurance marketplace. These plans must also offer the ten essential benefits, along with following the other rules dictated by the Affordable Care Act. Please note that if you purchase your plan outside of an exchange, you will not be eligible for any subsidies, such as the premium tax credit or cost-sharing reductions. Also, insurers do not have to offer coverage at all four metal tiers.

TIP

If you're shopping for private health insurance, off-exchange plans can give you more options and have potentially lower price points. Be sure that you understand the trade-offs, which we'll review on the next pages.

What are the different types of private health insurance plans?

All private health insurance plans, whether they are part of an exchange or not, work by partnering with networks of health care providers, as described above. And this is the important part, because the different types of health insurance plans are designed to meet different needs. Some types of plans restrict your provider choices or encourage you to get care from the plan's network of doctors, hospitals, pharmacies, and other medical service providers. Others pay a greater share of costs for providers outside the plan's network.

What are the basic network types for Marketplace and private exchanges?

The following are the basic types of health insurance networks:

Health maintenance organization (HMO)

HMO coverage is usually limited to care from doctors who work for or contract with the HMO. It generally won't cover out-of-network care except in an emergency. An HMO may require you to live or work in its service area to be eligible for coverage. HMOs often provide integrated care and focus on prevention and wellness. HMOs require you to choose a primary care physician in their network. All care is coordinated through the primary care physician, and you are required to get a referral to see a specialist. These plans feature lower copayments and usually have the lowest premiums.

Preferred provider organization (PPO)

A PPO allows you the most freedom when accessing your network of providers and using doctors and hospitals. There is a higher cost for using an out-of-network provider, but you are not required to get a referral to see a specialist. PPO plans usually have the highest premiums.

Exclusive provider organization (EPO)

An EPO is a managed care plan where services are covered only if you use doctors, specialists, and hospitals in the plan's network (except in an emergency). You can see a specialist without a referral, but out-of-network physicians are not covered at all. EPO premiums are generally less expensive than PPO premiums and more expensive than HMO premiums.

Point of service (POS)

Under a POS plan, you would select a primary care physician from an HMO-style network who will coordinate your care. You then also have access to a PPO network of doctors, hospitals, and other health care providers that belong to the plan's network. You are able to see out-of-network health care providers at a higher cost. POS plans require you to get a referral from your primary care doctor in order to see a specialist. Premiums are typically more expensive than "pure" HMOs and less expensive than PPOs.

TIP

If you go outside the HMO or PPO network of providers, you may have to pay a portion or all of the cost.

What about health insurance I get through my employer?

It is common for employers to provide health care coverage to their employees. This is also known as *group health insurance.* These are private plans purchased and managed by your employer. Employer-provided plans need to follow the same rules as other private insurance plans and cover the ten essential benefits. If you're eligible for an employer-provided plan, you do not need to purchase additional coverage through the marketplace. However, if your employer's plan costs more than 9.5% of your income or doesn't meet the ACA minimum coverage requirements, you might qualify for subsidized coverage on the federal or state marketplace (as applicable). Talk to your human resources department for more specific information about your plan.

What is COBRA?

If you have lost your group coverage from an employer as the result of unemployment, death of the insured (e.g., your spouse), divorce, or loss of dependent child status, you may be able to continue your coverage temporarily under COBRA, the Consolidated Omnibus Budget Reconciliation Act. You pay for this coverage. When one of these events occurs, you must be given at least 60 days to decide whether you wish to purchase the coverage. Learn more about COBRA on the Department of Labor website: https://www.dol.gov/general/topic/health-plans/cobra.

Public health insurance

Am I eligible for Medicaid?

If you're on a low income or tight budget, you should consider whether you qualify for Medicaid. Medicaid has eligibility requirements that are set on a state-by-state basis. It is a public health insurance plan primarily designed for those with low incomes and low levels of liquid assets. It's also designed to assist families and caretakers of small children in need.

What is the Children's Health Insurance Program (CHIP)?

The Children's Health Insurance Program (CHIP) is a federal and state insurance program similar to Medicaid; however, it is specifically designed to cover children below the age of 18. CHIP is primarily aimed at children in families who have incomes too high to qualify for Medicaid but too low to afford private health insurance. You can check whether you qualify for Medicaid and CHIP at https://www.healthcare.gov/medicaid -chip. Medicaid and CHIP can have separate names at the state level.

Do I qualify for a health insurance coverage exemption?

Most people must have qualifying health coverage or pay a fee for the months they don't have insurance. In 2017, the penalty is either 2.5% of your household income or $695 per adult and $347.50 per child, whichever is higher. If you qualify for a health coverage exemption, you don't need to have health insurance or pay the fee. Exemptions are available based on several circumstances, including certain hardships, some life events, health coverage, or financial status, and membership in some groups. All of the following are considered acceptable coverage to be exempt from the Affordable Care Act penalty:

- Individual or group health insurance plan (marketplace or private; grandfathered or not)
- Veteran's health care program (including Tricare)
- Medicare
- Medicaid
- The Children's Health Insurance Program (CHIP)
- Peace Corps volunteer plans
- COBRA continuation coverage

Exemptions are tied to the tax year during which you didn't have health coverage, not the year you fill out the exemptions application. To see if you're eligible for an exemption, visit https://www.healthcare.gov/health-coverage-exemptions/forms-how-to-apply.

HOW DO I MAXIMIZE THE VALUE OF MY HEALTH INSURANCE?

Maximizing value is considering trade-offs and what your potential need is. Health insurance is something you will probably use at least once a year if you get an annual physical. There is a good chance that you will use your health insurance more than that. Keep in mind that if you or a family member have an unforeseen medical event, such as a heart attack or stroke, you will require a significant amount of health insurance. For most of us, it's a question of when, not if, we'll use it.

Insurance companies use their own methods to calculate their premiums. Under the ACA, the factors are age, location, tobacco usage, individual or family, plan category (metal tier), and benefits additional to the essential list described earlier. States can limit how much these factors affect your premiums, and insurance companies cannot use gender, your current health, or medical history against you.

Even with the best health insurance plan, there are ways for you to optimize your health insurance coverage and get the best value, such as staying in your network, using the emergency room only for emergencies, maximizing your medication payments, comparison shopping for tests and procedures, using funds in your pretax spending accounts, getting preapprovals, and watching for billing errors. For details on these tips, visit my website.

Factors that determine the true cost of coverage beyond the premium

It is important to remember that the premium you pay is not the true cost of coverage, and it is important to calculate that true cost. Health insurance usually does not cover 100 percent of your costs. The following are the out-of-pocket costs that have an impact on your total spending:

Deductibles

The deductible is the amount of money that you pay out-of-pocket before your insurance company pays anything, with certain exceptions. A deductible is applied to the covered services first, so if you have a $1,000 deductible, you would pay for the first $1,000 of covered services. After you pay your deductible, your cost will usually be your copayment or coinsurance (see the following). Some services may not have a deductible. Family plans usually have a separate deductible for each person, along with a family deductible that applies to all family members. Generally, plans with lower monthly premiums will have higher deductibles.

Copayment

Your copay is a fixed dollar amount paid for each covered health care service. This is paid every time you use a service, so if you visit your physician monthly, you will pay it each time. These can vary for different services within the same plan, such as for medications and lab tests. Plans with lower monthly premiums will usually have higher copays.

Coinsurance

Coinsurance is the percentage cost of a covered health service after you've paid your deductible. For example, if you have coinsurance of 20% and a doctor's visit is $100, you would pay $20 out of pocket. Generally, plans with lower premiums will have higher copays.

Note: Covered services will have either a copay or coinsurance, not both, and may or may not have a deductible. You can find out the deductibles, copayments, and coinsurance for covered services, tests, and prescriptions with an insurance company's summary of benefits and coverage.

Out-of-pocket maximum/limit

This is the most that you would have to pay in a plan year for covered services. It is the sum of all the deductibles, copays, and coinsurance you pay each year. After you reach this amount, your health plan pays for 100 percent of covered benefits. This is important to calculate into your cost planning, especially if you have frequent health care needs. All high-deductible catastrophic marketplace plans have the same maximum. Usually the lower the monthly premium, the higher the out-of-pocket limit (which resets each year).

Allowed amount

Your allowed amount is the maximum a plan will pay for a covered health care service. This may also be referred to as an *eligible expense*, a *payment allowance*, or a *negotiated rate*. If a provider charges more than the plan's allowed amount, you may have to pay the difference. This practice is known as *balance billing*. A preferred provider may not balance bill you for covered services.

Note: The bottom line is that there will be a cost trade-off between premiums and the costs of care listed previously (deductibles, copayments, and coinsurance).

Should I consider a catastrophic health plan?

Catastrophic health insurance plans have low monthly premiums and a very high deductible (usually the maximum out-of-pocket limit, $7,150 for individuals in 2017). They may be an affordable way to protect yourself from worst-case scenarios, like getting seriously sick or injured. Catastrophic plans cover certain preventive services at no cost and at least three primary care visits per year. They cover less than 60 percent of your total costs of care, and you pay more than 40 percent. You also have to pay all other medical costs yourself until you reach your deductible. After that, the plan pays 100 percent of covered services.

Catastrophic plans are only available if you are age 30 or younger or if you qualify for a hardship exemption, and you cannot use a premium tax credit to reduce your monthly cost for a catastrophic plan. If you qualify for a premium tax credit based on your income, either a Bronze or Silver plan could be a better value. Be sure to compare.

What are my main considerations in choosing the optimal plan?

With health insurance, it's not just choosing the policy with the lowest premium. Consider your ongoing annual costs in terms of deductibles, copayments, and coinsurance combined with how many times you see a provider and the cost of your medications. And of course, make sure that all your providers, including specialists, are in-network and that your medications are covered. Also, see if you qualify for extra savings or subsidies through the Health Insurance Marketplace (Silver is the only plan that qualifies). Visit my website for a worksheet you can use to compare health insurance plans and calculate your annual outlay.

How will the ACA affect my taxes?

The ACA currently requires you to indicate health insurance coverage when filing a tax return. Details can be found on the IRS website at https://www.irs.gov/affordable-care-act/individuals-and-families/health-care-law-and-you.

How does the premium tax credit work?

The Affordable Care Act includes a premium tax credit. Per https://www.healthcare.gov, over eight in ten people who apply qualify for the credit and therefore pay lower premiums. When you apply for coverage in the Health Insurance Marketplace, you'll find out if you qualify. The amount of your premium tax credit depends on your estimated household income for the year. You can (and should) visit the IRS website for additional information about your own situation, to see if the premium tax credit is still available. Go to https://www.irs.gov/ACA.

Can I take a health insurance premium deduction?

You can claim a deduction for any premium that you directly pay for with after-tax money. You may not claim a deduction for any premiums paid by an employer. You also cannot deduct any subsidy (premium credit). Keep in mind that any deduction is subject to the medical expense limitation on income taxes.

WHAT STEPS DO I NEED TO TAKE TO APPLY FOR COVERAGE?

The first thing is to determine when can you sign up through the Health Insurance Marketplace. This will either be during the annual open enrollment or when you qualify for a special enrollment period. Open enrollment dates can be found on the healthcare.gov website.

If you qualify for insurance through an employer, you would enroll subject to their rules; some employers will start coverage immediately while others will have a waiting period. It is important to not terminate any individual coverage until your employer coverage is in effect so you have no gap in coverage and will not incur a penalty.

Are there exceptions to the open enrollment period?

You qualify for a special enrollment period if you've experienced certain life events, including losing health coverage, moving, getting married, having a baby, and adopting a child. If you qualify for special enrollment, you usually have up to 60 days following the event to enroll in a plan. If you miss that window, you must wait until the next open enrollment period to apply. Visit https://www.healthcare.gov for more information on special enrollment periods, including a complete list of qualifying events.

You can enroll in Medicaid and the Children's Health Insurance Plan (CHIP) any time of year, whether you qualify for a special enrollment period or not.

Job-based plans must provide a special enrollment period of at least 30 days.

How do I apply for coverage?

To apply for a Marketplace insurance policy, go to https://www.health-care.gov to complete your application. If your state has an exchange, you will be automatically directed to it when you fill out your home zip code. You can also apply over the phone, through the mail, or in person with a trained staff member. To apply, go to https://www.healthcare.gov/apply-and-enroll/how-to-apply.

If you are interested in individual health insurance (not through the Marketplace), you can apply directly with the company. Remember to check the Marketplace first so you don't miss any discounts or tax credits you may be eligible for.

IS MY HEALTH INSURANCE PERFORMING AS IT SHOULD?

During open enrollment (or special enrollment periods), you can renew your existing health insurance plan. If you are currently enrolled in a plan through the Health Insurance Marketplace, you will be automatically signed up for the same coverage each year unless you receive notification that your insurance company has left the Marketplace. Or you can choose a new plan. If you wish to make a change, you can do so during open enrollment for the federal and state insurance marketplaces, or if you qualify for a special enrollment period, you can apply during your exemption period.

Here are some reasons to consider getting a new plan or modifying your existing plan:

- To ensure that your premium is competitive
- You would like to change the metal tier on a Marketplace plan or the deductible, copayment, or coinsurance on a private insurance policy.
- Your insurance company has made changes to doctors and health care facilities that are included in their network.
- Your insurance company increases your copayment or coinsurance.
- Your pharmacy coverage has changed; this usually means that a medication you use is no longer covered.
- You've had a major life event.
- You've developed a chronic health care condition and have a high deductible, high copay, or coinsurance plan.

In this last case, you would want to try to lower your deductible and copay/coinsurance if possible.

Insurers are required to notify you in writing of any changes to coverage. For tips to keep costs down and to optimize your coverage, visit my website.

HOW DO I FILE A CLAIM?

Your medical provider will usually file a claim on your behalf with the insurance company. At the time of the visit, you should usually only be paying your copayment amount, although some practitioners have different arrangements or do not take insurance.

After your claim has been processed by the insurance company, you will usually receive an explanation of benefits (EOB) that can be confusing. It is important to review the EOB and ensure that it is accurate. The EOB will list the date of service, medical billing code (for each service), place of service, charge amount, allowed amount, not covered amount, reason code (why a service was not paid for), copayment or copay, deductible, benefit amount or percent covered, payment amount (amount paid by your insurance company to the provider), and amount due from the patient. According to the American Medical Association, 7 percent of medical bills in 2013 had errors, and some estimate that this is on the low side. Compare the EOB with the invoice from your provider. To learn more about the EOB components, spotting a mistake, and what you can do, visit my website.

TIP

Get preapproval from the insurance company prior to having any major procedures and non–medically necessary procedures.

WHAT COVERAGES WILL SUPPLEMENT MY HEALTH INSURANCE?

Basic health insurance does not provide coverage for all of your health care needs. The following are some additional products that you should consider.

What is dental insurance?

Dental insurance provides coverage for dental care. Dental plans are typically structured like health insurance plans, including dental HMOs and PPOs. Dental plans are usually offered through employers. You can also purchase dental insurance on your own, with premiums from $15 to $50 a month. Coverage usually has an annual maximum of $1,500, so it is not extensive. When reviewing plans, check if there is a waiting period before coverage starts and whether there are specific time limits for specific procedures and what the plan pays for, such as lab and material costs for crowns or bridges.

TIP

Be wary of dental discount programs. Dental discount programs are not dental insurance plans and provide discounts (savings) rather than insurance benefits. Some insurance companies offer dental discount programs rather than dental insurance.

What is vision insurance?

Vision insurance provides coverage for regular eye exams, eyeglasses, and contact lenses. Elective vision-corrective surgery may be covered under a vision insurance plan, but medically necessary major eye procedures, such as cataract surgery, are typically covered through health insurance plans. Vision insurance is often offered by employers. Premiums can range from $15 to $50 per month for individual policies. Be sure to compare the benefits provided.

Note: Vision insurance is currently included for children under the age of 18 in all health insurance plans.

What is gap insurance?

Gap insurance supplements your health insurance coverage by paying for out-of-pocket costs such as high deductibles. Please note that gap insurance plans are not regulated by the Affordable Care Act and therefore do not provide the same consumer protections. If you have a high deductible plan, you would be better off considering a health savings account.

What is short-term health insurance?

Short-term health insurance plans provide limited health care coverage for a temporary gap in insurance. These plans do not qualify as coverage under the Affordable Care Act, and for any time under which you're covered only by short-term health insurance, you will be considered "uninsured" according to the ACA mandate, and may incur a potential tax penalty. Short-term health insurance may have limits that regular insurance coverage does not have, such as caps on maximum benefits paid. The maximum coverage period is three months. However, you can purchase a new policy once the current policy terminates.

What should I know about spending accounts?

Health care and dependent care expenses can be a major part of your over-all budget. Fortunately, there are a few options that allow you to set aside pretax income to cover out-of-pocket expenses. Unfortunately, there are limitations to who can participate in these types of accounts and to what they cover. It is important to understand how each plan works, because they may be use-it-or-lose-it (i.e., if you don't use the money you've set aside in a given year, you will lose it) and often what is covered can fluctuate.

What is a flexible spending account (FSA)?

A flexible spending account (also known as a *flexible spending arrangement*) is a special pretax reimbursement account you put money into that you use to pay for certain out-of-pocket health care expenses. You don't pay taxes on this money. This means you'll save an amount equal to the taxes you would have paid on the money you set aside. These plans are only available if offered by your employer.

A wide range of medical expenses, including copayments, deduct-ibles, prescription medications, and medical equipment are covered. You cannot use your FSA to pay premiums. Please note that this is subject to change. For a current list of eligible expenses, visit the IRS website at https://www.irs.gov/pub/irs-pdf/p969.pdf.

Be careful, as you must project at open enrollment what your cov-ered care costs will be; and, subject to the options above, any money not spent will be lost.

What is a health savings account?

A health savings account (HSA) is a pretax reimbursement account that you can put money into that you use to pay for certain out-of-pocket health care expenses. You don't pay taxes on this money, so, like with an FSA, you'll save an amount equal to the taxes you would have paid on the money you set aside. These plans are only available to participants in a high-deductible health insurance plan. You cannot have any other health insurance, including Medicare Parts A or B.

An HSA can be used for medical expenses including deductibles, copayments, prescription medications, and medical equipment. Please note that this is subject to change; visit the IRS website at irs.gov and search for publication 502, "Medical and Dental Expenses," for a current list of eligible expenses.

An HSA is portable, so it remains yours if you switch jobs or insurance plans. The money can also be invested like a 401(k) plan strictly for medical expenses. Earnings are not subject to taxes. Any money used for qualifying health care costs is also not taxed. However, if the money is spent on nonqualifying health care costs prior to age 65, it is subject to taxes and a possible 20-percent penalty.

What is a dependent care flexible spending account?

A dependent care flexible spending account (DCFSA) is a pretax reimbursement account used to pay for dependent care services, such as preschool, summer day camp, before- or after-school programs, and child or elder daycare. These plans are only available if offered by your employer.

A DCFSA covers a limited list of dependent care expenses, including those listed above; overnight camps and private education are not covered. Please note that this is subject to change, and you should check with your DCFSA plan provider for a current list of eligible expenses.

Be careful; you must project at open enrollment what your covered dependent care costs will be, and any money not spent will be lost.

WHAT SHOULD I KNOW ABOUT MEDICARE?

Medicare is a federal health insurance program for Americans above the age of 65, along with people with certain disabilities. As of 2015, Medicare provided health insurance for more than 55 million people. Anyone above the age of 65, regardless of their income level, is eligible, provided that you have worked approximately 10 years before applying. A worker's spouse can qualify on the worker's record if they do not have enough credits of their own. It is important to note that Medicare consists of several components that eligible Americans can sign up for at different times; it is not one single service.

When should I sign up for Medicare?

Medicare requires you to sign up during a seven-month initial enrollment period, which starts three months before the month you turn 65 and extends three months after you turn 65. You can sign up after this time during the general enrollment period, which runs from January 1 through March 31 of each year.

Important: Because Medicare Part B does require you to pay premiums, you can elect to apply for only Medicare Part A. However, if you don't enroll in Medicare Part B during your initial enrollment period, you may have to pay a late-enrollment penalty for as long as you have Medicare Part B (your monthly premium will go up 10 percent for each 12-month period for which you were eligible). The exception is if you qualify for a special enrollment period.

If you want to know more about enrollment periods for Part B, please read the information about general and special enrollment periods on the medicare.gov website.

What is retiree insurance?

If you're retired and have Medicare and group health plan (retiree) coverage from a former employer, generally Medicare pays first for your health care bills and your group health plan coverage pays second. How your retiree group health plan coverage works depends on the terms of your specific plan. Your or your spouse's employer or union might not offer any health coverage after you retire, and if you can get group health plan coverage after you retire, it might have different rules and might not work the same way with Medicare. To learn more about retiree insurance, visit https://www.medicare.gov.

What if I am still working at age 65?

If you are age 65 or older, you or your spouse are still working, and you are covered under a group health plan based on that current employment, you may qualify for a special enrollment period that will let you sign up for Part B later. Find out more at https://www.medicare.gov.

Will my employer require that I sign up for Medicare when I turn 65?

If you are approaching age 65 and are still covered under an employer's group health insurance policy, you will need to consult with your employer's benefits coordinator to see if they require that you sign up for Medicare. If you are not required to sign up for Medicare, you can wait to enroll, though you'll need to qualify for a special enrollment period as noted previously. If your employer requires you to enroll in Medicare at age 65, you will be subject to the initial enrollment periods noted previously. In this situation, you can still keep your group health insurance coverage; however, health care charges are submitted to Medicare first, and any remaining costs will go to the group health insurance company.

How does Medicare work if I have other health insurance?

If you have Medicare and other health insurance or coverage, each type of coverage is called a *payer*. When there's more than one payer, coordination of benefits rules decide which one pays first. Tell your doctor and other health care providers if you have coverage in addition to Medicare. This will help them send your bills to the correct payer to avoid delays.

The insurance that pays first is called the *primary payer* and pays up to the limits of its coverage. The one that pays second is called the *secondary payer* and only pays if there are costs the primary insurer didn't cover. The secondary payer (which may be Medicare) may not pay all the uncovered costs. If your employer insurance is the secondary payer, you may need to enroll in Medicare Part B before your insurance will pay. The pay order refers to the *amount* of payment not the timeframe; it doesn't always mean the primary payer pays first in time, for example. If the insurance company doesn't pay the claim promptly (usually within 120 days), your doctor or other provider may bill Medicare. Medicare may make a conditional payment to pay the bill, and then later recover any payments the primary payer should've made. Find out which insurance pays first so you're not caught off guard.

What's a conditional payment?

A conditional payment is a payment Medicare makes for services another payer may be responsible for. Medicare makes this conditional payment so you won't have to use your own money to pay the bill. The payment is *conditional* because it must be repaid to Medicare if you get a settlement, judgment, award, or other payment later. You're responsible for making sure Medicare gets repaid from the settlement, judgment, award, or other payment.

If Medicare makes a conditional payment, and you or your lawyer haven't reported your settlement, judgment, award, or other payment to Medicare, you'll need to contact Medicare's Benefits Coordination and Recovery Center (BCRC). The BCRC will gather information about any conditional payments Medicare made related to your settlement, judgment, award, or other payment. If you get a payment, you or your lawyer should contact the BCRC, then the BCRC will calculate the repayment amount (if any) on your recovery case and send you a letter requesting repayment.

Can I apply for Medicare when I'm receiving disability benefits?

People who receive Social Security disability benefits and are covered under a group health plan from either their own or a family member's current employment also have a special enrollment period and premium rights similar to those for workers age 65 or older.

Which insurance will benefit me the most when I turn 65?

Employer health plans have become higher cost to the employee; we're now paying a greater share of the premium, higher premiums, higher deductibles, and increased copays and coinsurance. To see if Medicare is the better choice for you, consider which insurance will pay first, then consider the deductible and copay or coinsurance on your employer plan as compared to Medicare (with Medigap coverage; see below).

Should I consider dual coverage even if I'm at a small employer?

Usually not, because when you add up the combined premiums for Medicare Part B (covers medical services and supplies), Medicare Part D (covers prescription drugs), and your employer health insurance premium share, the total cost may be high. Dual coverage can make sense if you have a serious medical condition that is covered by your employer plan and not covered by Medicare. You should consider what the out-of-pocket cost or coverage gap would be if you don't maintain your employer coverage.

Can my spouse or other dependent stay on my employer's health plan?

It can make sense for your family overall if you remain on your employer's plan because it would be less expensive than if they sought out their own individual coverage. You can still sign up for Medicare. If you sign up for Medicare and decide to discontinue your participation in your employer's health insurance plan, your family may be eligible for COBRA coverage; you can confirm through your employer's benefits coordinator.

Can I continue my health savings account (HSA) when I turn 65?

If you sign up for Medicare Part A and continue to make HSA contributions, you will face tax penalties. Therefore, if you choose to remain in an employer plan that includes an HSA, do not sign up for Medicare Part A until you are no longer covered under the employer plan. Important note: If you file for Social Security retirement benefits any time after age 65, you are automatically signed up for Medicare Part A coverage up to six months retroactive to your Social Security signup date. If you made any HSA contributions during that six-month period, you would likely face tax penalties.

What are my coverage options under Medicare?

Medicare has four basic coverage plans, three of which offer traditional coverage (Parts A, B, and D) and an Advantage plan, which is Part C, as follows:

Medicare Part A (hospital insurance)

Part A covers services and supplies deemed medically necessary, such as lab tests, surgery, doctor's visits, inpatient hospital stays, skilled nursing facilities, hospice care, some home health care, and certain medical equipment (e.g., wheelchairs and walkers). This is the part funded by your payroll taxes, and so for most people, there will be no further premiums to pay. There is a deductible and various levels of coinsurance.

Medicare Part B (medical insurance)

Part B covers services and supplies needed to diagnose or treat your medical condition. Covered services include those that prevent illnesses such as the flu or that detect an illness at an early stage. Also covered are services such as an annual wellness check, clinical research, ambulance services, durable medical equipment, mental health services (inpatient, outpatient, and hospitalization), getting a second option, and limited outpatient prescription drug costs. Medicare Part B requires a premium.

With Parts A and B, collectively known as Original Medicare, you can go to any doctor, other health care provider, hospital, or other facility that's enrolled in Medicare and is accepting new Medicare patients, and you do not need to choose a primary doctor. You also do not need a specialist referral, but the specialist must be enrolled in Medicare. Most prescription drugs are not covered by Original Medicare, although there are a few exceptions. You can add drug coverage by joining a Medicare prescription drug plan (Part D). You generally pay a set amount for your health care (deductible) before Medicare pays its share. Then Medicare pays its share, and you pay your share (coinsurance or copayment) for covered services and supplies. There's no yearly limit for what you pay out-of-pocket.

For a list of variables affecting your Medicare out-of-pocket costs, visit https://www.medicare.gov.

Medicare Part C (Medicare Advantage plans)

Part C plans, also known as *Medicare Advantage plans*, are offered through private companies contracted through Medicare to provide Parts A and B benefits. They usually offer a drug plan as well. All Medicare Advantage plans cover you for emergency and urgent-need care. Some offer options such as an HMO's vision, hearing, dental, or health and wellness programs. The plans can choose to cover the costs of services that aren't medically necessary under Medicare. It's important to understand your coverages, limitations, and what you will pay out of pocket.

Medicare Advantage plans must cover everything that traditional Medicare does; however, the out-of-pocket costs can be higher than those from Medicare and Medigap policies combined. There are copayments for provider visits, hospital care, prescription drugs, and other care, but Medicare Advantage plans must limit your out-of-pocket expense to a set amount each year. Some plans will have lower out-of-pocket costs, and extra coverage for services such as dental, vision, and hearing benefits can be included.

Medicare Advantage plans have restricted networks of doctors and hospitals, while with Medicare you can visit any doctor or hospital that accepts Medicare patients. The lower-cost Medicare Advantage plans will usually have the smallest networks and higher out-of-pocket expenses. Your out-of-network outlay will be higher than the in-network out-of-pocket cost maximum.

Medicare Part D (prescription drug coverage)

An add-on coverage to Medicare, Part D is offered by insurance companies and other private providers. Some Medicare Advantage plans offer prescription drug coverage as part of their services. If you do not enroll in a drug plan once you are eligible and no longer have creditable coverage, you will be subject to steep and permanent financial penalties if you choose to enroll later. Part D requires a premium.

How do I enroll in Medicare?

To enroll in Medicare, you can apply on the Social Security website (https://www.ssa.gov/medicare) or follow the link through https://www.medicare.gov. There is no underwriting, just a short questionnaire.

You will be automatically enrolled if you are already receiving Social Security benefits and will receive your Medicare card in the mail three months before your 65th birthday.

What is Medicare supplement (Medigap) insurance, and will I need it?

Medicare, on average, covers about half of your health care costs, with the difference being paid out of pocket, by individual or group/employer health insurance, or through supplemental Medigap insurance. Medicare supplement insurance (Medigap) policies are sold by private health insurance companies and can help pay some of the health care costs that Original Medicare doesn't cover, like copayments, coinsurance, and deductibles.

Some Medigap policies also offer coverage for services that Original Medicare doesn't cover, like medical care when you travel outside the United States. If you have Original Medicare and you buy a Medigap policy, Medicare will pay its share of the Medicare-approved amount for covered health care costs, then your Medigap policy pays its share. To learn more about Medicare and Medigap, visit https://www.medicare.gov.

Warning: If you change your mind later and you have greater health care needs, you may not be able to purchase a Medicare Supplement plan. You can return to Medicare from January 1 to February 14 each year, which will allow you to continue Medicare Parts A and B. If more than six months have passed since you originally signed up for Medicare Part B, some states allow insurance companies to reject you or charge you additional premiums for Medigap coverage. The Affordable Care Act's prohibition against refusing or charging more to insure someone because of a preexisting condition does not apply to Medigap insurance companies. Some insurance companies also won't even provide Medigap coverage to those over the age of 70.

Most people should purchase Medicare Supplemental insurance, because Original Medicare likely will not cover all your needs. And the costs of not having Medicare Supplemental insurance could potentially derail your retirement or even send you into bankruptcy.

A Medigap policy is different from a Medicare Advantage plan. Those plans are ways to get Medicare benefits, while a Medigap policy only supplements your Original Medicare benefits. All Medigap policies are standardized, and a Medigap policy only covers one person. If you and your spouse both want Medigap coverage, you'll each have to buy separate policies.

If you decide to drop your entire Medigap policy, you need to be careful about the timing. For example, you may want a completely different Medigap policy (not just your old Medigap policy without the prescription drug coverage), or you might decide to switch to a Medicare Advantage plan that offers prescription drug coverage.

For a comparison table of Medigap plans, please visit my website. It's really important to compare the different plans to ensure you're getting the coverage you want. You can find a Medigap policy at https://www.medicare.gov.

Insurance companies may charge different premiums for the same exact policy. As you shop for a policy, be sure you're comparing the same policy (e.g., compare Plan A from one company with Plan A from another company). Be sure to compare the same type of Medigap policy as well. Also be aware of whether the insurance company uses medical underwriting or applies a different premium when you don't have a guaranteed issue right (also called *Medigap protections*) or aren't in a Medigap open enrollment period. Think twice about Medicare SELECT policies that may have lower premiums with the trade-off being a more limited choice of providers.

TIP

If you buy a Medicare Supplement plan within six months of enrolling in Medicare Part B, you can get any plan in your area, even if you have a preexisting medical condition. But if you try to switch plans after that, insurers in most states can reject you or charge more because of your health. It's important to pick your plan carefully. Some states do let you switch into certain plans regardless of your health, and some insurers let you switch to another one of their plans without a new medical exam. Find out about your state's rules and the plans available at your state insurance department website (http://www.naic.org/state_web_map.htm).

Beware "the donut hole"

A "donut hole" is a gap in coverage between when you reach a certain level of prescription drug expenses out of pocket (including your deductibles and copays) of $3,700 for 2017 and when you reach expenses of $4,950 out of pocket. Once you reach $4,950, the donut hole closes, and coverage kicks in again, and your drug plan will cover 95 percent of your costs for the remainder of the calendar year. While in the gap, for 2017, you paid 40 percent of the cost of brand name drugs and 51 percent of the cost of generics. These costs are declining until 2020, at which time you will pay a maximum of 25 percent while in the gap.

How do I file a Medicare claim?

If you're enrolled in Original Medicare, doctors and suppliers are required by law to file Medicare claims for the covered services and supplies you get. Find out which doctors in your area accept assignment for all Medicare-covered services. In special (and rare) circumstances, you may need to file a claim. Please consult the medicare.gov website for more information. If you have a Medicare Advantage plan (Part C), you won't have to file claims, because Medicare pays these private insurance companies a set amount each month.

TIP

The Right To Appeal: If you disagree with a coverage or payment decision made by Medicare or a Medicare health plan, you can file an appeal. The appeals process has five levels, and you can generally go up a level if your appeal is denied at a previous level. Gather any information that may help your case from your doctor, health care provider, or supplier. If you think your health would be seriously harmed by waiting for a decision, you can ask for a fast decision to be made, and if your doctor or Medicare plan agrees, a decision will be made within 72 hours.

How do I avoid fraud while I'm on Medicare?

Fraud is an issue with Medicare; however, there are some things you can do to stay safe, such as remembering that your health insurance information is confidential, so be careful about where you leave your health insurance card and who you show it to. Ask questions about services ordered by a medical provider, such as the need for a service and what the cost will be. If you don't feel that it's something you need, don't agree to the service. Medicare does not have official sales representatives; don't believe anyone who claims to be a Medicare representative.

CHAPTER 6

Homeowner's/Renter's Insurance: Selecting Your Tight End

"All men are created equal;
some work harder in preseason."
—EMMITT SMITH

The key to what all-time leading NFL rusher and Hall of Famer Emmitt Smith is saying is that anyone can show up at game time; however, you have to work hard and prepare in order to win. The time and effort that you put into choosing your homeowner's and renter's insurance policies will pay off when you need to file a claim. It's like the saying that you may only need a parachute once: When you need it, you'll be happy you have it.

DO I NEED HOMEOWNER'S INSURANCE?

If you own a home, you will need homeowner's insurance. And homeowner's insurance is almost always required by lenders, so you'll also need it when you buy a home. In the event of a disaster, if you don't have homeowner's insurance, your home would be left with little if any value. Homeowner's insurance pays claims for damages to your home, garage, and other structures, along with losses of furniture and other personal property due to damage or theft (both at home and away from home).

DO I NEED RENTER'S INSURANCE?

Most of us start out renting. If you are renting, your landlord's insurance coverage will not cover your possessions (the contents of your rental) in case of a fire, burglary, or other claim event. Renter's insurance is generally inexpensive and protects the things you own while also providing some liability coverage. Renter's insurance also helps you establish a favorable insurance track history (claims–loss history). This will help you with pricing and obtaining homeowner's insurance in the future.

What is usually covered under a homeowner's or renter's insurance policy?

On a homeowner's insurance policy, the key is to know exactly what is covered. If it is an all-risk policy, every event is covered except for listed exclusions. Here is what is usually covered:

- The structure of the home
- Separate structures on your property
- Personal property in storage.
- Personal belongings, such as furniture and other personal property lost to damage or theft, both at home and away
- Loss of use of the property
- Additional living expenses (ALE) if you have to leave your home because of an insured disaster
- Liability for bodily injury and property damage that you may cause to others through negligence and accidents in and around your home, as well as away from home, for which you are responsible
- Limited coverage for money, gold, jewelry, and stamp and coin collections.

What is a peril?

There are 16 basic perils that may be covered under a homeowner's policy. *Named perils* are events that are specifically covered under a homeowner's policy. Also, note that some peril coverage may be limited or not included in standard policies, especially these:

- Fire or lightning
- Windstorm or hail
- Explosions
- Riots or civil disturbances
- Damage caused by aircraft
- Damage caused by a vehicle
- Smoke damage
- Vandalism or malicious mischief
- Theft
- Volcanic eruption
- Falling objects
- Damage from the weight of ice, snow, or sleet
- Water damage from plumbing, heating, or air conditioning overflow
- Water heater cracking, tearing, or burning
- Frozen pipes or appliances
- Sudden and accidental damage from electric current

What may be excluded from a homeowner's policy?

Ask about exclusions. Many property policies on the market today exclude (i.e., will not pay for) certain types of damage. Ask your insurer, agent, or broker exactly what causes of loss and what items are not covered. If you want full coverage, make that clear to the insurance company in writing. Typical exclusions are listed below:

- Acts of war
- Construction defects
- Earth movement (shockwaves, sinkholes, landslides, mudflows, earthquakes)
- Floods
- Governmental action
- High-risk hazards (e.g., pools and trampolines)
- Home-based businesses
- Intentional losses
- Mold
- Neglect
- Nuclear hazard
- Ordinance or law
- Personal liability
- Pipe
- Power failure
- Sewer backups
- Termite damage
- Water damage
- Wear and tear

There are also specific items that may not be covered. Be sure to read your policy carefully to see if these items are covered or have a monetary limitation. If you would like additional coverage or if they are not covered, you can usually add a rider. Items that may need to be covered through a rider or other special coverage include the following:

- Antiques
- Art
- Cameras
- Coin collections
- Computers

- Jewelry
- Money
- Musical instruments
- Stamp collections

What type of homeowner's policy should I get?

You should look for a policy that covers your needs. For example, a policy classified as an HO-1 is a minimal policy that covers 10 of the 16 perils. An HO-2 protects against all 16 perils. HO-3 policies cover all 16 perils and typically insure your home and attached structures along with your belongings and your personal liability if you accidentally injure someone or damage their property. HO-4 is the tenant's form, for renters, and covers only belongings and personal liability. An HO-5 comprehensive form is the broadest form that you can get; it covers more perils than other types of policies. Just like an HO-3 form, an HO-5 is an open-peril policy form that can financially safeguard you against all perils unless your policy specifically excludes them in writing. HO-6 is for condominiums, and HO-7 is for mobile homes. Finally, HO-8 policies are for older homes and protect against all 16 perils.

How do I determine the basic coverage level?

Some important terms will help you determine the coverage level of your policy. As always, if you don't understand your coverage, ask your agent or company representative for further information.

Actual cash value

This phrase means that your policy covers the cost to replace what your property is worth at the time of your loss, less a deduction for depreciation (age and wear). This will provide you less coverage and is not recommended unless you have other substantial assets that could be used.

Replacement cost

This type covers the cost to replace your property and contents without any deduction for depreciation.

Guaranteed or extended replacement cost

This final category provides full replacement cost, even if that cost exceeds the coverage level.

HOW DO I MAXIMIZE THE VALUE OF MY HOMEOWNER'S INSURANCE?

Each insurance company uses its own method to calculate their premiums, which vary on a number of key factors that may include your home's location, the age and size of the building, the type of construction (materials), additional structures, local building costs, personal property, natural disaster risk, its proximity to a fire station, crime risk, property hazards, your credit/insurance score, and your claims history. For more details on these factors, visit my website.

TIP

Find the right company to fit your needs, personal profile, and X factors. And don't forget to review how to choose an insurance company to find a stable insurance company that will be around to pay your claim.

How do I optimize my premium?

Be sure to review with your agent or company exactly which discounts you may be eligible for. Keep the following tips in mind as you consider different policies.

Consider a higher deductible

Increasing your deductible by just a few hundred dollars can make a big difference in your premium, however your deductibles may also generally be higher for certain events, such as windstorms and hurricanes.

Insure your house, not the land under it

After a disaster, your land is still there. If you do not subtract the value of the land when deciding how much homeowner's insurance to buy, you will pay more than you should.

Confirm that dwelling coverage is the same when comparing proposals

Some insurers estimate the amount of dwelling coverage needed and then automatically add an extra 25 percent or more of protection to make sure you're covered in the event of a total loss.

Check for limits on increased living expenses in the event of a claim

Some companies will set a limit equal to 30 percent of the dwelling coverage, while other companies will have no limit and will instead reimburse you for actual living expenses for one year.

If you have an older home, does the insurance company cover costs to bring old systems up to code during a rebuilding process?

Some insurers include this in the policy for no additional premiums, while other insurance companies will charge a sizeable premium for this coverage.

Automatic payment discount

If you pay your premium by automatic deduction from your bank account, you can save 5 to 10 percent.

Bundling

Purchasing multiple types of insurance through one insurance company can lead to savings. Usually this includes homeowner's and auto insurance and can include other types of coverage. Be sure to compare buying the policies separately to make sure that the discount is worthwhile. Discounts can reach up to 30 percent.

Claim-free discount

If you haven't had a claim in a certain period, you may be eligible for discounts up to 20 percent.

Protection devices and safety improvements

Protection features, including burglar alarms, deadbolt locks, fire extinguishers, smoke alarms, carbon monoxide detectors, sprinkler systems, storm shutters, and fire-retardant roofing material can earn you discounts of up to 15 percent.

Insurance companies typically have an overall limit on how much a policy can be discounted—usually a total of 30 percent—so be sure to compare your options.

TIP

Make an inventory of all your personal property, along with a photograph or video of each room. Save receipts for major items and keep them in a safe place away from your home. This will be helpful if you have to make a claim. There are a few apps to help you with this. I'd recommend the NAIC app Scr.APP.bk for your inventory as you take photos and add notes.

HOW DO I MONITOR MY HOMEOWNER'S INSURANCE?

As with any financial asset, it is important to monitor your homeowner's insurance to ensure that it still meets your objectives.

The following are items to review annually on your homeowner's (or renter's) insurance policy or if you move to a new property:

Deductible

Raising your deductible is the best way of keeping your premium affordable without reducing your protection.

Make sure that you have the right amount of coverage

Ensure that you have enough coverage by purchasing guaranteed or extended replacement coverage to make sure that your coverage is keeping up with current replacement costs. Look at current replacement costs.

Some events call for an immediate review of your homeowner's insurance coverage:

- You acquired expensive possessions (or got rid of them) or the value has changed significantly.
- You've gotten or no longer have a dog; dog bites are one of the top reasons for homeowner's insurance liability claims.
- You started or ended a home-based business.
- You installed a home security system or other safety feature upgrade.
- You remodeled or added on to your home (or outbuildings).
- You began renting out a room or your home (your insurer could claim you are running a business).
- Your risk changes, such as adding a swimming pool or getting a trampoline.

In many states, insurance companies must file any rate increases with the resident's state insurance department, subject to their approval.

The insurance companies must justify that the rate increase is necessary. However, this varies by state insurance department.

HOW DO I FILE A CLAIM?

The need to file a homeowner's insurance claim can often come at the worst possible time; you may not even be able to live in your home. Despite that, you need to start the claim process as soon as possible. Below are some steps that will help you during the claims process.

Review your policy

Be sure to understand what is covered and what is not covered. For example, if you have a homeowner's policy that pays additional living expenses (ALE), go ahead and ask your insurance company for payment.

Prepare documentation of your loss

Document everything that occurs during a loss: take photos, write down the narrative; collect receipts, contracts, and appraisals; and document phone calls (including the name of anyone you speak with). Document the details of all damaged items, including their date of purchase and approximate value (receipts are great if you have them). Most insurance companies will require a written inventory.

Do not discard damaged items or materials without checking with your insurance company

The adjuster will need to see your damaged items to make a proper evaluation. If you are required by a governmental body to discard an item for safety reasons, be sure to take photos and save the details of who required the item to be discarded.

Document the claim process

No detail is too small. Thorough recordkeeping is important if you want to receive the maximum value on a claim. Note the name, title, and contact information of everyone you speak with about your claim, along with the date, time, and issues discussed.

Secure your property to mitigate damage

The insurance company will require you to take reasonable care of your property and to do what you can to prevent further damage. Insurance companies refer to this as *mitigating damage*. If you can't stay in your home, turn off your power, gas, and water to prevent further damage. Other examples would be covering holes in the walls and roof to protect from the elements or moving property that is at risk of further damage.

Arrange for housing

If your homeowner's or renter's policy includes *loss of use* coverage, your insurance company is required to offer you rent or hotel costs, regardless of where you stay, even if it's a family member's home.

Hire a public adjuster

A public adjuster will act as your advocate. They are familiar with insurance policies and will work to support your interests and will help you negotiate better settlements with your insurance company. Make sure that your public adjuster has a current license with your state insurance department. Be aware that a public adjuster typically receives an average of 15 percent of your settlement.

Wait for approval from the insurance company before doing anything

You should always wait for the insurance company's claims adjuster before having any work done; otherwise, you may be responsible for those costs.

Continue to pay your insurance premiums

Keep paying your insurance premiums, unless you have a type of coverage that allows you to stop paying premiums, such as disability insurance.

Close the claim only when you're ready

With a homeowner's claim, there might be additional occurrences down the road, so do not close your claim until you are sure.

As with other types of insurance, you should generally not file a small claim, but in the event of a significant loss, you'll be glad you did.

TIP

Be on the lookout for those who will try to take advantage of you after a major event such as storm, earthquake, or other natural disaster. The most common type of homeowner's insurance scams are from "storm chasers," people who visit areas recently struck by strong storms or other natural disasters. They will offer to perform repair work; however, they either don't actually do the work or do a poor job that can leave you worse off than before they started.

WHAT ARE SOME RELATED COVERAGES?

The following coverages can be added to a homeowner's policy if they are relevant to your needs.

Building code upgrade

This rider covers the added cost of rebuilding your home to meet current building standards.

Inflation guard

This automatically adjusts your homeowner's coverage to reflect increased construction costs.

Jewelry

Jewelry is covered under a basic policy to a certain specified limit, not the appraised value. If the value of your jewelry exceeds the basic limit, you'll need more coverage.

Personal possessions coverage limits

Homeowner's policies generally pay a standard percentage of the dwelling coverage to replace your damaged, destroyed, lost, or stolen personal property. If your possessions have a higher value, you should do an inventory and be sure to add coverage for them through a schedule or rider.

Separate structure coverage

This type of coverage is for structures such as barns and garages.

Sewer back-up coverage

Sewer coverage can be purchased separately above and beyond what your basic homeowner's insurance policy covers. Homeowners and business owners are responsible for the maintenance and repair of their house or sewer lateral, which is the pipeline between the city sanitary sewer main, usually located under the street, and the building.

What is umbrella insurance?

Personal liability insurance, also known as *umbrella insurance*, provides additional coverage to losses that exceed the limits of other policies. It is a cost-effective way to increase your liability coverage by $1 million or more, in case you are at fault in an accident or someone is injured on your property. It supplements the insurance you already have for home, auto, and other personal property.

What should I know about condominium insurance?

Potential and current owners should review their condo agreement and the state statutes to determine the duties and insurance requirements for the owners and for the association. If you own a condominium (or co-op), you will need to consider and review two insurance policies:

Coverage you obtain as an individual

Your individual policy covers everything in your condominium (or co-op), such as kitchen cabinets, built-in appliances, plumbing, wiring, bathroom fixtures, and items not covered in the group policy. This would include any property that you are solely responsible for that is considered "residence premises," such as a garage, storage unit, patio, or balcony.

Coverage purchased by your condominium (or co-op board)

The board policy covers common areas of the property that are shared with other owners, such as the roof, stairs, hallways, recreational facilities, basement, elevator, boiler, and sidewalks. This coverage may also extend to covering a unit up to its bare walls, floor, and ceiling. Key question: Is your coverage *walls in* or *walls out*? You need to know to ensure you have no gap in coverage.

How do I know if I'm walls in or walls out?

The terms *walls in* and *walls out* are a way to designate what the unit owner is responsible for. *Walls in* is when the unit owner has to provide coverage only for carpeting, painting, washers, and dryers inside the unit. If the unit owner also has to provide coverage for pipes and wiring between the walls, then coverage is *walls out.*

As an owner, you will be insured through Unit Owners Insurance Form ISO HO 00 06, whereby the phrasing of the policy form adapts to the agreement between the unit owner and the association (and if coverage is walls in or walls out). Usually anything that the insured is required to insure is covered. This is coverage A.

Loss assessment is an additional coverage. This covers the amount the association would charge the unit owner for damage to property owned by all members collectively. The loss must be from an insured peril—other than earthquake or a volcanic eruption. The limit on this coverage is $1,000, regardless of the number of assessments per loss. Additional coverage (a limit increase) can be obtained by adding endorsement HO 04 35 Loss Assessment Coverage. Also note that assessments that are the result of actions of a governmental body, such as a code violation, are not covered.

Personal property coverage

This includes all of the contents of your home, such as computers, furniture, televisions, furniture, clothes, bicycles, other electronics, and everything else. Add up the cost to replace all of your major items, and you'll find a dollar value that would be hard to come up with out of pocket. It also covers damage to other renters' belongings and structural damage. Renter's insurance even covers property stolen from outside your home—for example, an iPad stolen from your car or a hotel room.

Liability coverage

Liability insurance covers you if someone is injured in your home. This would cover medical costs and also protect you in a lawsuit. This coverage can extend beyond your home.

Additional living expenses (ALE)

ALE coverage pays for temporary lodging if you can't stay in your home after a claim event such as a fire or burst pipe.

What are some of my other considerations with renter's insurance?

Look around

As with all other types of insurance, you should get multiple quotes from different companies. Compare on an apples-to-apples basis.

Increase the liability limit

Most renter's policies come with $100,000 of liability coverage. And while this may seem like a lot, it usually isn't. I recommend liability coverage equal to your assets. An additional $500,000 of coverage is usually about another $20 a year in premiums.

Consider flood insurance
Water damage from a flood is usually not covered under a renter's policy. Flood insurance can be purchased through the National Flood Insurance Program (NFIP).

It's inexpensive
According to the National Association of Insurance Commissioners, the average annual premium for a renter's policy is $188 (in 2016).

What should I know about earthquake insurance?
Earthquakes are a major concern for those who live in the Pacific Earthquake Belt, part of which runs up the West Coast, from Southern California to Alaska. Per the US Geological Survey, about 81 percent of the world's biggest earthquakes originate from this area. Earthquakes do happen in other states, so even if you're not on the West Coast, you may still want to consider it.

Homeowner's and renter's standard insurance policies do not cover earthquake damage and other types of earth movement, such as landslides and sinkholes. Earthquake coverage will fill that gap.

Earthquake insurance usually has three parts:

- Dwelling coverage, for your home
- Personal property coverage, for the items in and around your home
- Additional living expenses (see previous)

What discounts can I get with earthquake insurance?
You may be eligible for a discount if any of these criteria apply:

- Your home has been built or retrofitted to reduce the impact from an earthquake or ground movement.

- You have a wood-frame house rather than brick or masonry.
- You've added sprinklers in your home.
- You've installed metal straps to the walls and roof.

Premiums are higher in areas where there is a greater risk of an earthquake, such as California, and earthquake insurance premiums can exceed the cost of your homeowner's insurance policy. Earthquake coverage can be offered either as a separate policy or as a rider to your homeowner's insurance policy. In California, earthquake insurance is mostly purchased from the California Earthquake Authority through major insurance companies.

What are common exclusions on earthquake insurance policies?

Common exclusions on an earthquake insurance policy include fire, damage to your land and vehicles, and flood.

How do I file a claim for earthquake damage?

If you notice damage or just suspect it, report it to your insurance company as soon as possible. Your insurance company is required to open a claim when notified, and if they refuse to do so, you can contact your state's department of insurance. Request that a claims adjuster come out as soon as possible and show them all the damage while making sure they inspect hidden areas of your property. An insurance company can deny claims that are not reported within one year, either from when you notice property damage or from when you *should* have noticed it, if you had looked carefully.

What is flood insurance?

Homeowner's insurance does not cover flooding. Homeowner's insurance covers damage that occurs from water falling from the sky but not water coming up from below. So, if a storm takes off your roof, you have a homeowner's claim; if your home is damaged because the nearby stream overflows, you would only have coverage through a flood insurance policy. Flood insurance covers you from all types of flooding, including damage due to groundwater seepage, mudslides, a water main break, and even a neighbor's aboveground swimming pool collapsing.

Flood insurance is available to homeowners, renters, condo owners and renters, and commercial owners and renters. Homes and businesses with mortgages from federally regulated or insured lenders that are in high-risk flood areas are required to have flood insurance. Flood insurance is not federally required if you live in a moderate- to low-risk flood area, but it is available and is recommended.

How are my rates set for flood insurance?

Rates are set nationally and are the same with each company and through any agent. The rates depend on multiple factors, including the date your home was built, the type of construction, and your property's flood risk. Flood risk levels are divided into three categories:

- High-risk areas have at least a 1-percent chance of flooding annually.
- Moderate-to-low-risk areas have less chance of flooding annually; however, the risk of flooding still exists. Per the NFIP, 20 percent of flood claims originate from these areas.
- Undetermined-risk areas are where flood-hazard analysis has not been conducted but a flood risk exists.

The average flood insurance policy premium is $700 a year. Your premium will depend on the factors above, the amount of insurance, and what is covered. The average residential flood claim from 2010 to 2014 through the NFIP was $39,000.

What is covered by flood insurance?

All policies provide coverage for buildings and contents. The standard policy pays for direct physical damage to your insured property up to the replacement cost or actual cash value (ACV) of actual damages, or the policy limit of liability, whichever is less. Policies cover structural damage, including damage to a furnace, water heater, air conditioner, flooring, and debris clean up. There is limited coverage for basements, crawlspaces, and ground-level enclosures on elevated homes. It's important that you review what restrictions there might be on a policy. Also, nonessential contents such as computers, furniture, and televisions are not covered under a standard flood policy. Flood insurance only covers damage that is a direct result of flooding and does not cover the actual land.

Flood insurance is typically purchased as a separate policy or as an optional rider on your homeowner's policy, typically through the National Flood Insurance Program. The NFIP maximum coverage is $250,000 per dwelling and $100,000 for contents, with lower limits available. Over the last few years, some private insurance companies have begun offering flood insurance, either as a stand-alone policy or as a supplement to the NFIP coverage.

TIP

Typically, there's a 30-day waiting period from the date of purchase before your policy goes into effect. That means now is the best time to buy flood insurance.

Visit the NFIP website at https://www.floodsmart.gov for flood maps (and how to understand them), coverage information, policy rates, and a flood insurance agent locator.

What about home businesses and offices?

This can be a confusing area, so you should carefully review your policy to see what is covered and what is not covered. You should also speak with your agent to make sure that all of your activities are fully disclosed.

What if I have a home office?

If you have an office outside of the home, your home office should be covered under your homeowner's policy. This would include business equipment and materials, which are typically covered up to $2,500.

What if I have a home business?

If you fail to notify your insurance company, you will potentially place both your business and your home at risk. An undisclosed home business can result in a claim being denied, whether or not the claim involves the business. For example, if your home is burglarized, a claim on any stolen personal property could be denied by the insurance company, stating that the burglars were lured by the uninsured and undisclosed home business. This could also result in your homeowner's or renter's policy being canceled.

Injuries sustained on your property by a person present due to your business are also not covered. This would result in you being personally responsible for medical costs and damages. This includes customers and even delivery service personnel, such as USPS, UPS, and FedEx. Business data stored at home may not be covered either.

The following are the three levels of coverage that you should consider. Keep in mind that coverage options will vary somewhat by state and by company and will be dependent on your business and your risk exposure.

Basic coverage

Determine if you can add a policy rider or endorsement to your existing homeowner's insurance policy. This will usually increase your coverage from $2,500 up to $5,000–$10,000. You can also add a liability endorsement if you receive visitors at home.

In-home business policy

Coverage can be added as an endorsement to an existing homeowner's or renter's insurance policy or as a stand-alone insurance policy. Based on your desired coverage limits and your type of business, you may have to opt for a stand-alone policy, as the endorsements will usually be more limited. An in-home business policy will protect you from loss of or damage to equipment, such as computers and other electronic devices, documents, and business property, along with limited coverage for merchandise kept in inventory for resale purposes, off-site property, and a loss of income if you suffer a disaster or fire that shuts you down. These policies will usually provide liability coverage for up to three employees working in your home. This type of policy is recommended for low-income, low-risk, and part-time businesses due to the limited coverage.

Standard business owner's policy (BOP)
A BOP would provide broader coverage and would be similar to insurance for a business outside the home.

What if I use a home-sharing service?
If you decide to rent out your home to a third party, you will no longer be covered under your traditional homeowner's insurance policy. If you are renting out your home, you are running a business, even if it's through a home-sharing service or peer-to-peer rental site such as Airbnb, VRBO, and HomeAway. You'll need home-business coverage.

If you plan on frequently renting out a room or your entire home, a separate landlord policy may be your best option. This will cover your home, property contents such as appliances and furniture, and lost rental income due to building damage, legal fees, and liability protection.

Insurance companies have also started to offer an endorsement to cover a homeowner for certain situations, such as if a renter destroyed or stole your personal belongings. The endorsement is designed to fill in some of the potential personal property protection gaps in a typical homeowner's insurance policy for customers who occasionally rent out their homes to temporary renters. Coverage can extend to personal property up to $10,000 per rental period, subject to your deductible with limitations and exclusions.

A few home-sharing services do offer some form of host protection, with guarantees to cover disputes between owners and renters. There are also other limitations, exclusions, and restrictions that decrease the value of this protection, so be sure to read the details.

> **TIP**
>
> Consider renting only to guests who show proof of homeowner's, renter's, or personal liability insurance. Therefore, if a guest damages your rented property, you can report a claim on the guest's policy.

What if I'm a guest of a home-sharing service?

If there is damage to your belongings during your stay, your own homeowner's or renter's policy should protect you, similar to when you rent a hotel room. Be advised that the services have user agreements that reserve the company's right to make a claim under your policy for any damage or loss you cause to an accommodation.

> **TIP**
>
> Review the terms of use every time you participate in a home share; they can change at any time. It is likely that there will continue to be changes as these services become more solidified and experience is gained.

What is moving insurance?

Moving companies and homeowner's insurance will cover some damages or loss of property; however, there are significant coverage gaps. Moving companies will usually offer some type of valuation coverage.

For example, the coverage will differ if you pack a box or if the moving company packs for you. Even if you notice damage or loss after reaching your destination, you are legally bound to pay the moving company. You must then follow the claim procedure and file an insurance claim in order to get compensated. Visit my website for more information.

CHAPTER 7

Life Insurance: Selecting Your Kicker

"We get one opportunity in life, one chance at life to do whatever you're going to do, and lay your foundation and make whatever mark you're going to make. Whatever legacy you're going to leave; leave your legacy."
—RAY LEWIS

There have been talented players who couldn't make it in the NFL because they were not able to work hard enough or stay focused. Ray Lewis was the 26th pick of the 1996 draft. Countless forgotten players were drafted before him, some only active a few seasons. Through hard work and dedication, Lewis overcame personal issues to succeed and left a legacy in which he's seen as a leader and a fan favorite.

Creating a lasting legacy takes hard work and dedication. Part of the legacy we leave is how we take care of the ones we love. A sound part of any lasting financial plan is life insurance, used strategically. Life insurance is not necessary for everyone, and your choices in purchasing and maintaining your policy will dictate the legacy you leave.

DO I NEED LIFE INSURANCE?

The purpose of life insurance is to provide income to someone who is financially dependent on you, including a spouse, a domestic partner, children and other dependents, and business partners. It is meant only to supplement the loss of your income for your loved ones for a specific period and a specific purpose.

The type of life insurance you need depends on the length of time your coverage would replace your income, which, in turn, depends on what expenses need to be covered. For instance, most people have a set number of years they need life insurance to cover, such as 30 years to protect a mortgage and 18 years to provide for a child.

It's important to remember that life insurance is about risk protection. Life insurance is often purchased for the wrong reasons; your policy is a tool for financial leverage—nothing more, nothing less. It's not an investment and not a retirement account. To know whether you need life insurance, you need to know *why* you need it.

Do I need life insurance for my children?

No. Remember that life insurance is about replacing the income of someone that you are financially dependent *on*, not that of someone who's dependent on you. Unless you are the parent of a child entertainment star, you almost certainly will not be dependent on your child's income, so they do not need life insurance.

HOW MUCH LIFE INSURANCE DO I NEED?

There are as many ways to determine how much life insurance you need as there are people to ask this question of. The methods range from the simple to the exceedingly complex. Even choosing a method that you feel makes the most sense for you leaves the issue that you are trying to hit a moving target: Your needs change all the time, so you also have to monitor your coverage.

The accuracy of any calculation depends on the method chosen, as well as the information used. Your needs will have to be adjusted at certain milestones, such as children graduating from college, retirement, moving, and so on. Along with calculating future income and expenses, you will also need to estimate your life expectancy. There is no one right method; however, if you don't understand the calculation, you probably shouldn't use it. For most people, the simplest methods are often the best.

Below are three straightforward ways to calculate your need:

Multiple of income

This method uses a multiple of—typically, five to eight times—your annual income. While simple, this earnings-multiple method misses a range of important factors. For example, it ignores household demographics (e.g., number of children), past savings, Social Security offsets, housing expenses, taxes, etc. It also ignores expected life changes and individual preferences about sustaining the living standards of survivors. This is a "best guess" method.

Annual + one-time – assets

Another method is to add your annual needs and your one-time needs then subtract your current assets. The following graphic provides an overview of this method.

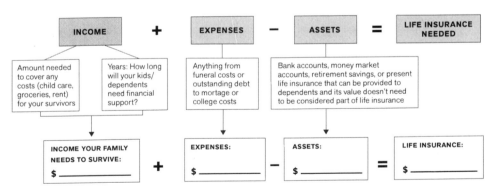

Example:

Jack, 35, has two kids (ages 4 and 7) and makes $80,000. He wants to buy a 15-year term policy to cover his kids in case anything happens. He plans to leave his family $80,000 a year until his children are in college and can provide for themselves. The income his family will need for the next 15 years is calculated below.
80,000 × 15= 1,200,000

Jack also plans to leave his family 10,000 for his funeral costs and 120,000 for both his kids to get a college education (2016's average tuition was 60,000 for public school and 142,000 for private). These are his lump-sum expenses:
($60,000 × 2) + $10,000 = $130,000

He estimates an annual expense of $20,000 for his rent, $1,000 for his yearly credit card bills, and $1,000 for his insurance fees.
$20,000 + 1,000 + 1,000 = $22,000

His assets include a $50,000 IRA, $25,000 money market, and $25,000 savings account. These monies are subtracted from the life-insurance calculation because this isn't money he needs to factor into his policy—it's money he can already provide for his family.
$50,000 + $25,000 + $25,000 = $100,000

Jack needs this much life insurance:
$1,200,000 + ($130,000 + $22,000) - $100,000 = **1,252,000**

Capital preservation

With this approach, the death benefit is used for income replacement, and the beneficiaries live off the income it produces. The death benefit (the principal) is invested and left intact. If this sounds like the right approach for you, estimate the annual income that would be needed by your beneficiaries. Next, divide this figure by the assumed after-tax rate of return (a conservative estimate is best) that could be earned on the invested principal.

annual income (replacement) ÷ after-tax rate of return = insurance benefit

For example, for an annual income need of $100,000 (after taxes) and an assumed after-tax rate of return on the principal (death benefit) of 5 percent per year, the replacement need would be $2,000,000 ($100,000 divided by 5 percent, or .05).

$$\$100,000 \div .05 = \$2,000,000$$

The amount of money needed to fund income replacement is typically greater than other methods, as the beneficiaries are intended to live off of income only. This method is ideal in situations where replacing the income lost due to the death of a breadwinner is the primary concern. However, this method only factors in the replacement of the income and does not take into account any lump sum needs at the time of death. In addition, a client's financial situation might be more complex and may even require additional analysis. For example, the issues of funding a college education, integrations with Social Security benefits, paying the estate tax, and determining other sources of income are not included in this method.

TIP

A spouse or domestic partner who does not have earnings (or has lower earnings) still contributes economic value and may have a life insurance need. Consider the costs of replacing the value added such as childcare, cooking, and house maintenance.

Visit my website for more information on calculating how much life insurance you should have and for a downloadable worksheet.

CHOOSING A LIFE INSURANCE PLAN

There are two basic types of life insurance: term life and permanent life (also called *cash value* policies).

What is term life insurance?

Term life insurance provides coverage for a specified period of time and does not accumulate a cash value. Following are the basic types of term life insurance:

Annual renewable term (ART)

Also known as a *yearly renewable term* (YRT), the annual renewable term features an annually increasing premium and a level death benefit, which means that the payout is the same at any time during your coverage.

Level premium term

These policies feature a level premium for a specified number of years (the premium may or may not be guaranteed for the entire level premium period). At the end of this period, either the policy will terminate or the premium will commence to increase annually at a significant rate (usually prohibitively high). Currently, this is the most popular type of term insurance and usually the most suitable, as it pegs your need to the specific time period.

Decreasing term

Sometimes known as *mortgage insurance* because it's often used for mortgage cancellation in the event of your premature death, decreasing-term insurance features a level premium and a decreasing death benefit, meaning that the payout decreases over time.

Return of premium term

A return of premium term allows you to receive the sum of premiums paid (sometimes with interest) after a certain number of years, usually the end of the level premium period.

What is permanent life insurance?

Think of a permanent life insurance policy as a bucket into which you pour liquid money. The bucket has a spigot at the bottom, and the company turns the spigot to drip money out of the bucket to pay for the expenses associated with the policy, such as the cost of insurance, mortality expenses, overhead, and other policy-specific fees. Meanwhile, the money left in the bucket earns interest at a rate declared by the company. It's your responsibility to keep enough money in the bucket (by making adequate, timely premium payments) to pay the policy expenses as they come due.

Since there are many unique products available in the marketplace, be sure that you are making a valid "apples-to-apples" comparison between policies. Evaluating any type of permanent coverage can quickly become a complex and daunting task. Today's permanent life policies are so complex, with so many moving parts, that elaborate sales illustrations are essential. Keep in mind that most life insurance illustrations are based on projections rather than on guarantees.

Understanding how all the components of a permanent (cash value) life insurance policy interact is integral to understanding how and why the policy performs as it does. When a policy is issued, the company is at risk for the entire death benefit. That's because the early premium payments go to cover mortality and other expense charges, leaving little or nothing to apply to the cash value. When a cash value starts to accumulate, this gradually reduces the company's net amount at risk.

For example, we'll use a policy issued for $100,000. When it is issued, the entire $100,000 is at risk to the insurance company. The cash value of the policy acts as a reserve account, reducing the amount at risk to the insurance company. Therefore, if the cash value in the 30th year of the policy is $60,000 at a certain point, then the net amount at risk to the insurance company is $40,000 ($100,000 of death benefit less the $60,000 of cash value).

Here are the four basic components that determine how the policy will perform:

Earnings

Earnings impact the increase of a policy's cash value and the policy's overall performance. Following are the various types of earnings for different permanent (cash value) life insurance policies.

Dividends

Dividend are used for earnings on participating whole life insurance policies and are declared by the insurance company at their discretion (dividends are not related to any financial measure). For tax purposes, dividends are considered a return of a portion of the premiums paid for the policy. When the policy is purchased, the policy owner can elect a form of dividend option, and most insurers allow the dividend option to be changed once the policy is in force. The most common dividend options are payment in cash, reduce premium, leaving dividends with the insurer at interest, buying paid-up additional insurance, buying additional one-year term insurance, and repaying policy loans (some whole life policies may not offer all of these options).

Interest Rates

Used for earnings on universal life policies and interest-sensitive whole life insurance policies. Interest is usually credited on the accumulated value after policy expenses (mortality/risk charges and overhead expenses) have been deducted, so the actual return is less than the credited rate.

Index crediting rate

On equity-indexed life insurance policies, earnings are based on the rate of return of a certain equity index (or indices). Earnings are therefore dependent on the performance of the selected index (or indices), the participation rate, and type of crediting method selected. These policies usually also include a guaranteed, fixed investment option.

Subaccount return rate

On variable life insurance policies, there are two types of accounts. The first is the fixed account, and this account earns interest at the current rate. The other type is a variable account, whose earnings or losses are the net gain or loss from amounts invested in the investment subaccounts.

What are mortality charges?

The mortality charge is the cost of pure life insurance protection, based on experience tables developed by actuaries and on actual mortality experience. It is the amount the company charges the policy owner periodically for the insurance element in the policy. Each company determines its own mortality charges based on these tables and other factors. Mortality rates are not disclosed on some policies.

What administrative and overhead expenses are charged?

Overhead expenses include all the operating costs that a life insurance company incurs in the course of doing business. These costs fall into four basic categories: cost of facilities, data processing, employees (labor), sales expenses (includes commissions, marketing costs, sales offices). These expense factors will vary widely with every life insurance company.

What is persistency?

Persistency is a measure of how long a life insurance company's policies are staying in force (active).

The factors listed above can adversely affect the long-term performance of your life policy and are usually at the discretion of the insurance company. Results can vary—and they certainly will. Dividend and interest rates tend to change the most and can impact the performance of a policy. However, a small change in mortality rates will have a greater impact on the policy performance, although this does not occur very often. Illustrations typically highlight projected earning rates and estimate policy values in future years. Think of the illustration more as a convenient way of showing how the policy works than as a reasonable estimate of future values. Life insurance policies are complex and need to be analyzed with care.

Keep in mind that life insurance companies generally do not like to divulge details about their products in terms of their components and consider this proprietary information.

What are my options for permanent life insurance?

There are many different types of permanent life insurance. Following are the most common:

Whole life insurance

A whole life policy has a level death benefit and a fixed premium while paying dividends. Dividends are not guaranteed and depend on the company's actual investment return. Dividend options typically include increased cash value, cash, the purchase of fully paid-up life insurance (additions), a premium reduction, increased cash value, and a purchase of one-year term insurance.

Universal life insurance

Also known as *flexible premium life* or *adjustable life* insurance, universal life can have a level death benefit or an increasing death benefit. The premiums are scheduled to be level; however, they can be paid at any time, in any amount (up to certain limits). These policies will build up a cash value and allow for policy loans and partial withdrawals. This premium flexibility does cause issues, because if sufficient premiums are not paid, the policy will terminate.

Guaranteed universal life

These policies guarantee the death benefit if all scheduled premiums are paid in full when due. These policies may or may not accumulate a cash value; they are designed to provide coverage past age 95 or 100 and up to age 120. They function as a lifelong term life insurance policy, where you have the option to accumulate a cash value. A note of caution: If you miss a scheduled premium or pay less than the total premium due, you may lose the guaranteed death benefit.

Equity-indexed universal life

Equity-indexed universal life (EIUL) is a newer form of universal life insurance that is extremely complex and combines elements of variable life (see following section) into the mix. The main difference between this and a traditional universal life policy is in how excess interest is credited. Most EIUL policies have two separate accounts that can be used to credit interest. One account has a fixed interest rate that is declared by the insurance company periodically. The second account provides an equity-index option that offers you the opportunity to earn rates of interest based on positive equity (stock) market returns. However, the cash value of the EIUL policy is not exposed to losses due to negative market returns.

The amount of interest credited to your cash value is tied to the performance of the policy's particular equity index. Companies use a range of indexes that include the S&P 500, the Dow Jones Industrial Average, the Lehman Brothers Bond Index, and FINRAAQ. In years where the index performs well, the interest credited to the policy's cash value rises, and in years where the index performs poorly, the interest rate falls. Typically, EIUL policies guarantee that the interest rate will never fall below zero so that the policy won't lose money if the stock market index declines.

The first thing to watch out for is that these policies usually have a cap or limit on the amount of interest that can be credited to your policy. Therefore, if the cap is 10 percent, and the index return is 14 percent, you will only earn 10 percent. The insurance companies can, at their discretion, also adjust what is called the *participation rate*, so that a policy owner receives a lesser percentage of the total return. For example, a company may offer a 100-percent participation rate guaranteed for the life of the policy. If the policy has an 80-percent participation rate, and the policy has a cap of 10 percent, the most you will ever earn on the policy is 8 percent (80 percent of 10 percent). There are also different indexing methods that are used in measuring the market return, which you should understand before signing a policy.

Variable life and variable universal life
Variable policies earn interest on a portfolio of investments that you, as the policy owner, choose from a selection offered by the company. The policy may be surrendered for its cash value at any time, subject to a surrender charge. The cash value and death benefit of your policy are not guaranteed, although some policies do guarantee that the death benefit cannot fall below a minimum level.

If your portfolio does well, the earnings on the cash value of your policy may exceed what you would have earned through a standard universal life policy; however, if the performance of your portfolio tanks, you'll have to put in additional funds to keep your policy in force. That can get pricey and could endanger your policy.

There are multiple fees associated with these, including federal and state premium taxes (average of 3 percent of premiums), mortality and expense (M&E) charges assessed against cash values (ranging from .6 to .9 percent), and asset management charges (from .2 to 1.6 percent).

Joint-survivor (second to die) life insurance
Joint-survivor life is a type of coverage that can be a part of any type of permanent cash value policy. This type of coverage insures two people (usually spouses) and pays a benefit only at the second death. It's used primarily for estate-planning purposes, as the estate tax is usually only payable at the second death.

Should I choose term life insurance or permanent life insurance?
The bottom line is that you need to be able to make this decision on your own, and the key is to become educated. Rather than starting with the

question of whether one type is better, consider whether you need life insurance and how long you will need its coverage. Many people do not have anyone who is financially dependent on them, and for those who do, their need is usually for a set period of years. Any need for a permanent policy is usually offset by the accumulation of other assets.

There are some situations where a permanent life insurance policy, such as guaranteed universal life, makes sense: when you have a permanent need that will not be offset by the accumulation of other assets. Life insurance is also commonly used to offset potential estate tax liabilities.

Should I purchase life insurance through my employer?

If you've ever worked for someone else, you've probably been offered term life insurance at either a flat amount of coverage or a multiple of your salary as part of your benefits package. You might have also been offered the opportunity to purchase additional coverage for yourself and for your loved ones and dependents.

This type of insurance is called *group life term insurance*, because the particulars of your policy depend on the company's pool of policyholders. This affects your choices of policy, the benefits, and various other factors. The premiums typically increase over time, either annually or every fifth year (at age 30, 35, etc.). Coverage is usually also not *portable*; in other words, if you leave the employer, your coverage is discontinued.

If you are in good health, purchasing additional life insurance coverage through your employer—beyond what your employer may offer and pay for—is almost always more expensive over any long period than purchasing an individual policy on your own. The *underwriting*— the process of determining the rate you pay based on the level of risk you pose—is not selective with group-based policies; the group must cover all employees to a certain extent, and this leads to higher premiums. Although individualized underwriting is generally required if you decide to purchase more than a basic amount of coverage through the group plan, the rates you pay still must account for the generalized risk the insurance company is taking on by covering the group.

TIP

Based on current tax law, any premiums that your employer pays on coverage over $50,000 is classified as taxable income. Please consult your tax advisor to confirm and to determine your options.

Many corporate benefit programs offer life insurance that doesn't require a physical exam or medical tests. Although the policy amount you can purchase is often capped, it is a way to get some coverage if you are unhealthy and fear you can't afford the premium. Becoming a member of an association or organization also often allows you access to a group life insurance policy.

Some employers offer group universal life insurance (or similar type of coverage). This coverage is usually portable and may offer the option to accumulate a cash value. Consider whether you need this type of coverage and, even if your employer is paying, what the reportable taxable income will be.

If I'm in the military or a veteran, should I purchase life insurance through the VA?

The Department of Veterans Affairs (VA) offers life insurance programs for veterans, service members, and their families. There are also voluntary programs in place that ensure the survivors of retirees (and, in some situations, active duty members) continue to receive income throughout their lifetimes.

If you are a member of the military, be skeptical of presentations; there has been a long history of financial abuse. Be sure that you are purchasing coverage you need and understand.

WHAT ARE SOME ADDITIONAL COVERAGES THAT I CAN ADD TO A LIFE INSURANCE POLICY?

A policy rider is an optional benefit that can be added to a policy for an extra premium. Legally, it is defined as a document that amends the policy or certificate. It may increase or decrease benefits, waive the condition of coverage, or otherwise amend the original contract.

Accelerated death benefit

This rider allows payment of a portion of the face amount before your death if you're diagnosed with a terminal illness or injury. This rider is automatically included on a number of new policies and has been retroactively added to some in-force policies.

Accidental death benefit

This rider provides a benefit in addition to the face amount of a policy, payable if you die as a result of an accident.

Annual renewable term

An *annual renewable term rider* is used to "blend" term life insurance into a whole life policy, which will reduce the premium and reduce the cash value.

Child rider

A *child rider* provides insurance coverage for your children.

Cost of living

A *cost-of-living rider* allows you to purchase one-year term insurance equal to the percentage change in the consumer price index with no evidence of insurability.

Disability rider

A *disability income rider* typically pays you a monthly benefit of 1 percent of the death benefit in the event that you become permanently and totally disabled.

Long-term care

A *long-term care insurance rider* provides access to cash value to cover eligible long-term care cost. If you use these riders, they will reduce the cash value and death benefit of your policy. The terms may be more restrictive and the benefits less than on an individual long-term care insurance policy; for example, they usually do not have an inflation option.

Other insured

An *other insured rider* allows you to insure an eligible family member or if coverage is related to a business, other eligible business partners/employees.

Spousal rider

A *spousal rider* insures your spouse and domestic partner. This may vary by local and state regulations.

Terminal illness

A *terminal illness rider* (also known as a *living benefits rider*) allows you to collect part of your life insurance benefits prematurely to pay for medical care in the unfortunate event of a catastrophic disease or illness.

Waiver of cost of insurance

A *waiver of cost of insurance rider* waives the cost of insurance in the event that you become totally and permanently disabled (universal life insurance policies).

Waiver of premium

Under a *waiver of premium rider*, your premiums are waived in the event that you become totally and permanently disabled before a specified age.

Keep in mind that each carrier may only offer certain riders per policy and may offer different riders than those listed above. And don't decide to add any rider too hastily. Remember, many of these riders are more profitable for the insurance carrier than for you as the insured.

What is simplified issue life insurance?

Simplified issue policies are also marketed as *no exam* policies. While it is true there is no medical exam, there is usually an extensive medical questionnaire and more stringent health qualifications. These policies work well for those in good health who wish to skip the medical exam. Premiums will typically be higher than a fully underwritten life insurance policy with limits on the maximum available death benefit.

What is guaranteed issue life insurance?

Guaranteed issue policies do not require any medical exams or health questions. Premiums will be higher since the life insurance companies cannot make any risk assessment. These policies have age limits and lower maximum death benefits.

What is graded death benefit life insurance?

A *graded death benefit* is typically sold to seniors, although some policies are available to those at any age. The premiums are high, and the death benefits are a lot lower than comparable plans that make use of medical underwriting. The policies will typically pay only a fraction of the full death benefit for the first year or two of the policy. They are worth considering if you are not able to get coverage elsewhere and you absolutely need life insurance coverage. It's better to have this coverage than to not have any, and it can be replaced if and when your health issues improve.

What is term laddering?

Term laddering is a strategy where you purchase multiple term policies with different guarantee periods to meet different needs. For instance, if you have a specific ten-year need (e.g., covering college costs), you would purchase a ten-year guaranteed level premium policy. If you also had a twenty-year need (e.g., income for your spouse) you would also purchase a twenty-year guaranteed level premium term policy. If you have multiple life insurance needs that span different time frames, term laddering may help you get all of the coverage you need and still control costs.

What should I consider in naming a beneficiary?

A beneficiary is the person you designate to receive the funds in your policy in the event of your death. You can name both a primary and a contingent beneficiary and, if you wish, multiple primary and contingent beneficiaries. The death benefit goes to the contingent beneficiary in case your primary beneficiary is also deceased.

How you choose your beneficiary (or beneficiaries) will depend on your situation and on the laws of your state. I'm not an attorney—always check with legal counsel if you want to be sure—but I do know these basics: Life insurance proceeds typically avoid probate and are distributed straight to your beneficiary and are usually not subject to income tax but may be subject to estate taxes.

TIP

Don't forget to name a contingent beneficiary. If the primary beneficiary passes away before the insured and there is no contingent beneficiary named, the life insurance proceeds would become part of your estate.

Who should I name as policy owner?

Choosing a policy owner is a process quite similar to choosing beneficiaries. Typically, you are the owner (at least in community property states). I am not as familiar with how this works in separate property states, because my practice has been limited to community property states, but you can learn more on your state's department of insurance website.

HOW DO I MAXIMIZE THE VALUE OF MY LIFE INSURANCE?

Each insurance company uses its own method to calculate premiums, which vary by gender, age, marital status, medical issues, financial health, occupation, avocations, and hobbies, among other factors. For more details on these factors, visit my website.

How do I optimize my premium?

Each insurance company has its own pricing strategy. Companies also have different perspectives on medical and health issues; some companies are more lenient. Following are five of the best ways to save on life insurance:

Research your policy

Begin a month or two ahead before buying. It won't be as sexy as buying a new car or an electronic gadget, but the work will likely save you money, rather than just going with the first insurance agent you meet.

Exercise

In general, healthy people pay less for coverage.

Know your medical history

If you're familiar with your health and medical history, you'll be in a far better position to make a case for your application.

Wait for health issues to stabilize

Some health issues may cause you to have to sit tight for a few months (or even a year) until an insurance company will agree to sell you a life policy. If you have a complex medical condition, consider working with an experienced insurance agent. Find one who has experience with medical conditions or other situations like yours or at least has access to multiple life insurance companies. They can advise you on how a condition will be interpreted by a particular provider.

Shop around

Look around at different companies, especially if you have a health condition. Rates for specific health conditions will vary significantly from company to company, so use an online term life quote service. If you are looking at permanent life insurance quotes, be sure that they are an "apples-to-apples" comparison.

What factors affect my premiums?

Whether you've chosen the term route or the permanent route, one thing's for sure: Your health and your medical history—even the physical shape you're in once you apply for a policy—are going to play a major part in determining how much you pay for life insurance. And in some cases, your financial situation may also come into play.

The life insurance industry is making it more and more difficult to figure out what premium is obtainable. Most advertised quotes are for so-called best-available rates, which are available to only a very small percentage of potential buyers. The next higher rate classes can reflect a significant jump in premiums (25 percent plus).

Life insurance companies use ten basic criteria for determining premium classifications in addition to major health issues. These criteria are treated differently by each company and will cause varying premiums. Here are the main factors:

- Your height/weight ratio (BMI)
- Your tobacco usage
- Cholesterol
- Blood pressure
- Family history
- Driving record
- Foreign travel
- Participation in dangerous sports or hobbies
- Alcohol or substance abuse
- Your occupation

In reviewing a specific health issue, insurance companies will also consider the following factors as relevant:

- The age of onset or first symptoms
- Years since diagnosis or final treatment
- The severity of the health issue
- Hospitalizations
- Frequency of doctors' visits
- Prescription medications

- Changes in prescribed medication or dosage
- Family history
- Any other health issues

How will major health issues affect my life insurance?

As anyone with a serious health condition may know from shopping for life insurance, finding coverage at reasonable rates, if at all possible, is difficult. Poor health equates to a bigger risk for insurance companies, which pass the cost on to customers. Some insurers specialize in certain coverage; in one extreme situation, I had a client with a heart condition history who was declined by one company but offered a preferred rate by another. You shouldn't assume that a specific health issue will preclude you from obtaining life insurance coverage; the insurance companies will factor in the severity and whether you have it under control.

Insurance companies use rating classes that can range from best available to table ratings, which can add either a flat amount per thousand dollars of coverage or multiply the cost of insurance. The insurance companies use various names for their underwriting classifications as well, so focus on the premium you will pay and not the rate class. Be patient, don't give up, and shop around—because the odds are in your favor that you'll eventually be able to find a company that will take a chance on you.

For a list of some common health conditions that will raise your insurance premiums and possibly make obtaining life insurance challenging, visit my website.

TIP

When it comes to the underwriting process, honesty is the best policy. Don't fib or omit, even though you think you might be able to get a better rate if you do. And here's why (apart from the ethical considerations): It could come back to bite you and your beneficiary. Your coverage will likely be dropped, and you could even be prosecuted for fraud. It's not worth the risk.

What financial information may be taken into consideration?

If you are considering large amounts of coverage or if the insurance you are requesting is tied to a business, insurance companies will likely ask you questions about your financial life. This is called *financial underwriting*. What the company will be looking for is an insurable interest, meaning that there is a specific need or financial logic for the coverage. If someone who makes $45,000 a year requested coverage of $10 million, the insurance company would question the insurable interest.

Can I have temporary life insurance coverage while my policy is in underwriting?

In some cases, when your life insurance application is taken and you've tendered an initial premium payment, you'll receive a *conditional receipt*, which binds your life insurance coverage effective on the date of your application, provided the underwriting process determines that you're eligible for the coverage for which you applied. That means that even if you die in an accident the day after your application is submitted, your beneficiary will be awarded the death benefit for which you applied. But if the reason you suddenly die is in any way related to an undisclosed medical condition—known or unknown—that's discovered in the underwriting process, your beneficiary will not receive the death benefit.

MONITORING YOUR POLICY

Policies are living things and there are many components that can affect their performance. This is particularly true with permanent policies that build cash value over time. For example, if you've taken out policy loans or have a permanent cash value life insurance policy, such as universal life, variable universal life, equity-indexed universal life, or interest-sensitive whole life, these all require vigilant attention to premium payments and the investment portfolio. You'll want to be aware of how much money it'll take to keep those policies in force and whether you can afford to keep them going. Term insurance, on the other hand, is a little less complicated.

The perfect amount of life insurance today may not be the right amount tomorrow. Therefore, as with all financial assets, it's a good idea to review your coverage needs every so often, especially if you have a major life change such as having children, children graduating from college, retirement, and changing careers. Consider whether your life insurance coverage is consistent with your current needs both in terms of the amount and the type of coverage.

Why should I monitor my permanent cash value life insurance policies?

If you have a cash value life insurance policy, especially one purchased more than ten years ago, your policy has a very high chance of terminating without value. To avoid this unwanted outcome, higher premiums are needed on almost every older universal life policy (traditional universal life, variable universal life, or indexed life)—basically, on any life insurance policy where the premiums are not fixed. And if your premium is guaranteed, such as on a whole life policy, you may be required to pay premiums for significantly longer than you expected—or you'll find yourself receiving a lower cash value than you'd anticipated.

TIP

Life insurance companies are not required to disclose whether your policy is underfunded and that higher premiums may be required or that they have decreased the interest rate or increased the cost of insurance. You can compare annual statements to see a change in interest rates, and a few companies do indicate when a policy is projected to lapse, although this is not the norm.

A change in mortality costs, which used to be rare, is becoming more common. Multiple companies announced in 2016 that they would be increasing their mortality costs. Unfortunately, details are rarely provided. A tick in the interest rate has much less impact than an increase in mortality rates.

Over the next few years, policies are going to continue to implode with it coming as a shock to the policy owner. It is not unheard of for the premium required to continue a policy to double, triple, or even quadruple—especially if premium payments are missed. Missed premium payments exacerbate the issue, even though this has been a key selling point for policies.

Policy loans can also cause issues with a policy. If excessive loans are taken out, the policy can terminate. You would then not only be faced with losing your policy, but you could also have a phantom income tax gain.

How do I find out how my permanent (cash value) life insurance policy is performing?

How a policy was originally set up doesn't matter; what's happened since a policy was put into place is what matters. The only way to determine the impact of changes in the policy components is through an *in-force illustration*, a projection of values based on your current cash value and the company's current interest rate/dividend scale/earnings, cost of insurance (mortality expense), and overhead charges.

If you have a life insurance policy, you should make sure that you review your policy by ordering in-force illustrations from your agent or company. The longer you wait, the greater the chances of an unpleasant surprise. You should request, at minimum, two in-force illustrations:

- One based on your current premiums and interest rates, dividend scale, projected earnings, cost of insurance (mortality costs), and expense charges

- One for the premium required to endow the policy at maturity based on current assumptions as listed in the previous bullet

Along with the in-force illustrations, you should also request a current statement of values to include the death benefit, accumulated value, net cash surrender value, cost basis, and—if there's a policy loan—the loan balance, annual loan interest, and loan interest rate.

For a free guide on how to get details from the insurer, including a form letter to send to your insurer asking for the information, you can go to my website: http://Tonysteuer.com/insurance-annual-review-guides.

TIP

When requesting an in-force illustration for a variable life insurance policy or an equity-indexed policy, use a conservative (low) rate of return.

You can also request in-force illustrations reflecting different scenarios, such as a reduced death benefit that would continue to maturity based on your current premium, different dividend options on a whole life policy, number of years that premiums are required, and loan pay-off scenarios. Sometimes you might request these additional in-force illustrations after receiving the initial ones. While the new premium may be quite higher than the originally planned premium, the sooner it's caught, the better; this issue will compound.

What should I do if my policy is not performing as expected?

Your options will depend on the type of policy you have. Whole life policies may allow for dividends to reduce or pay your premium (lowering your out-of-pocket costs). Universal life policies will allow you to reduce the death benefit so you can pay the same premium or increase the premiums to maintain the current death benefit (within limits). Consider a reduced paid-up policy; this would allow for no further premiums and would result in a lower death benefit and cash value.

You can surrender the policy; this can result in a taxable gain, which is typically calculated by subtracting the cost basis (usually the sum of premiums paid) from the value received (such as surrender value, loans, withdrawals, dividends). The insurance company should provide an estimate of the taxable gain on request. If you no longer have a life insurance need, you can transfer the net cash surrender value to an annuity. Be careful here, and be sure to read up on annuities. Finally, you can sell the policy on the secondary marketplace, also known as a *life settlement*. A life settlement company might be willing to buy your whole or universal life insurance policy from you for more than its cash surrender value. This company will continue paying your premiums so that it can eventually claim the death benefit, or it might sell your policy to a different company, which would then take over the payments and claim the benefit.

TIP

If you have no need for a cash value, which is often the case if you have a permanent life insurance need, consider whether you can exchange your policy for a guaranteed universal life policy, which will lower or sometimes even end your premiums while offering a guaranteed death benefit. The trade-off is that guaranteed universal life policies usually have minimal if any cash value.

What should I consider before replacing a life insurance policy?

Replacing an in-force life insurance policy can be a very good idea or a very bad one. It depends on many factors. Dealing with the complexities of life insurance replacement is like peeling away the layers of an onion. Remove several layers, and there are still many layers remaining. *Replacement* means discontinuing one life insurance policy to purchase another. A very fine line divides *replacement* (which is permissible under state insurance law) from *twisting* (which is prohibited by state law), replacing a life insurance policy primarily for the agent's benefit, to earn a new agent commission.

When you consider replacing a life insurance policy, you should weigh the pros and cons. A new life insurance policy will have a two-year incontestability provision and a two-year suicide provision. It's important to not terminate your existing insurance until you have received and accepted the new policy to ensure that it is what you were expecting. You can download a life insurance policy comparison worksheet from my website.

In today's world, the words *caveat emptor* have never been more true. Because of the cash value element and its complexities, it is much more difficult to analyze a permanent life insurance policy in a potential replacement situation. There are many types of different permanent life insurance policies. For this section, we will use the generic term *permanent life insurance* to mean any type of life insurance that builds up a cash value, including whole life, universal life, variable life, variable universal life, equity-indexed universal life, and all variations on each of these policy types.

Illustrations should never be the sole criteria for evaluating a replacement. Illustrated cash values and illustrated death benefits are never reliable predictions of future results. More information is needed. At a minimum, you should attempt to find out what the underlying assumptions are for the in-force illustration on the current policy and for the sales illustration for the proposed policy. You should be aware that there might be differences in the assumptions used by each company, which may render a comparison invalid. Make sure you are comparing apples to apples.

What are the dangers of my using a policy loan?

Policy loans can be a useful short-term option when immediate cash is needed, but they are not the long-term solution so widely proclaimed. In fact, policy loans (available with most forms of permanent life insurance) are one of the most complex, misunderstood, and misused components of a life insurance policy. Out-of-control policy loans can erode a life insurance policy over time, eventually draining the death benefit—and saddling you with a substantial (phantom) income tax bill.

Policy loans are more complicated than agents sell them to be, with promises of premium-free life insurance. Borrowing to pay premiums reduces the death benefit. Some companies today even suggest to clients with underperforming policies that a policy loan could support their faltering policy. But this robs Peter to pay Paul, and the policy owner eventually must make up the difference. Life insurance policies also have different types of policy loans. Read more about the pitfalls of policy loans on my website.

What is an IRS Section 1035 tax-free exchange?

Typically, on the surrender of a life insurance contract, a gain is immediately recognized by the policy owner to the extent the value received exceeds the policy owner's cost basis in the transferred policy. *Value received* typically consists of surrender value and any previous withdrawals or loans. *Cost basis* is typically the sum of premiums paid and can be requested from your insurance company.

Section 1035 allows certain exchanges of life insurance to be made without an immediate recognition of gain. The tax that otherwise would be imposed on a lump sum disposition of certain life insurance policies (and annuities) can thus be postponed. Generally, a contract received in a 1035 exchange carries over elements of the original contract in addition to cost basis.

LIFE INSURANCE AND TAXES

The general rule for calculating an income tax gain on a life insurance policy is to subtract the basis (usually sum of premiums paid) from the total value received (usually the surrender value and any outstanding loan).

WHAT IF I'M SERVING AS TRUSTEE ON AN IRREVOCABLE LIFE INSURANCE TRUST?

If you are serving as a trustee on an irrevocable trust, you are responsible for the management of the life insurance policy held in the trust. Trustees have a fiduciary responsibility to ensure that the policy (or policies) is being managed properly and will provide the expected benefits. To learn more about your fiduciary responsibility, read "A Duty to Advise" on my website.

WHAT HAPPENS IF THERE IS NO CLAIM MADE ON MY LIFE INSURANCE OR I NEED TO TRACK DOWN A POLICY?

Lack of communication can cause problems. The insurance company doesn't pay out a claim until they're notified that somebody has passed away, so if the beneficiary doesn't know about the policy, the death benefit might not be paid for some time. Or the uninformed beneficiary might never claim the money, which then could become part of as much as roughly $1 billion in life insurance benefits that has gone unclaimed in the United States. Visit my website for a checklist of tips for finding life insurance policies.

CHAPTER 8

Long-Term Care Insurance: Lining Up Your Defense

*"If you are prepared, you will be confident,
and you will do the job."*
—TOM LANDRY

S uper Bowls are usually won or lost because of great defenses. While most of us focus on the offense, the core indicator of a winning team is usually their defense. Yes, there are certainly exceptions to the rule; however, teams with a good offense and a great defense will usually beat a team with a great offense and a good defense. And the key to a good defense is preparation, hard work, and planning ahead. Defense is about doing the little things that usually go unnoticed. Coach Landry is known as one of the greatest NFL coaches of all time and is a member of the Pro Football Hall of Fame. He was known for his preparation and innovation.

Planning for your retirement falls into the same category of doing the little things that will go unnoticed for decades, until you retire. Long-term care insurance is about preparation. It is insurance that you purchase usually decades in advance of possibly needing it. It often goes unnoticed and yet can play a critical role in a successful retirement plan. Long-term care insurance coverage pays for expenses that are not covered by health insurance or Medicare.

WHY DO I NEED LONG-TERM CARE INSURANCE?

Unless you plan on passing away before age 65, there is a high chance that you will need some type of long-term care. One of the largest projected costs for the average American in retirement are medical expenses, with estimates approaching a total of $250,000 or more. Long-term expenses are the real wild card, as they are uncertain and can range from nothing, if you're exceptionally healthy, to over $1 million. A costly long-term care event could quickly disrupt an effective retirement plan.

Long-term care covers personal needs commonly known as the *activities of daily living*, such as severe cognitive impairments (more than 50 percent of claims), bathing, dressing, eating, continence, toileting, and transferring. These are all part of the aging process. Sometimes these needs may be short-term, such as if you were to break a hip, or they may be long term, with a chronic condition such as Alzheimer's disease. Inevitably, the longer you live, the more likely you are to need some type of long-term care.

Besides the activities of daily living, you may need assistance with everyday tasks, sometimes referred to as the *instrumental activities of daily living*, including housework, managing money, taking medication, preparing and cleaning up after meals, shopping for groceries or clothes, using the telephone or other communication devices, caring for pets, and responding to emergency alerts such as fire alarms.

Around 70 percent of people turning age 65 will need long-term care insurance, and women are more likely than men to need coverage: They outlive men by about five years on average. If you live alone, your odds are higher, especially for in-home care, as there will be no spouse or partner to help you with the activities of daily living. If you have a chronic illness or had an accident that caused a disability, your odds will go up even more. Your family history will indicate a higher likelihood; how did your parents fare in their later years? Poor diet and exercise habits will also increase your chances of needing long-term care insurance.

The following table shows that, overall, more people use long-term care services at home (and for longer) than in facilities:

DISTRIBUTION AND DURATION OF LONG-TERM CARE SERVICES

Type of Care	Average number of years people use this type of care	Percent of people who use this type of care
Any Services	3 years	69%
At Home		
Unpaid care only	1 year	59%
Paid care	Less than 1 year	42%
Any care at home	2 years	65%
In a Facility		
Nursing facilities	1 year	35%
Assisted living facility	Less than 1 year	13%
Any in-facility care	1 year	37%

Source: US Administration on Aging

Keep in mind where you plan to live in retirement. Retirement communities with their own long-term care facilities are gaining in popularity and some of these eliminate the need for long-term care insurance, since the cost of the long-term care facilities are included in the overall cost; but there are some communities that will require a long-term care policy or will provide a discount if you have one. If your plan is to stay in your home, you will need to consider long-term insurance unless you are wealthy enough to self-insure (i.e., save your own money to pay for health care expenses).

What are the types of long-term care that I may need?

When you are looking for long-term care insurance, just as with any type of policy, consider what your needs will be. There is a wide variety of long-term care options on the spectrum, including the following types:

Home health care

For eight out of ten people, the preference (and reality) is that care occurs inside a home, according to the Congressional Budget Office. Examples of home care services include an unpaid caregiver, who may be a family member or friend; a nurse, home health, or home care aide;

or a therapist who comes to the home. There are many businesses that offer varying levels of in-home care.

Adult day services (and community centers)

Adult day services include social activities and assistance with activities of daily living, provided during the day to individuals who otherwise reside at home. Approximately half of the individuals who take part in adult day services have some form of dementia, according to the National Adult Day Services Association; therefore, adult day services frequently focus on cognitive stimulation and memory training. Medicare may cover adult day services in certain limited instances but generally does not.

Skilled nursing facility

Skilled nursing care usually includes medical care and rehabilitation services. Medicare covers, in full, the first 20 days of care in a skilled nursing facility following a qualifying hospital stay (defined as three days in a row in the hospital as an inpatient). For days 21–100 in the facility (again, following release from a qualifying hospital stay), you must pay a copayment, which is often covered by your supplemental health-insurance policy, while Medicare covers the remainder of the cost. Medicare does not cover the costs of care in a skilled nursing facility beyond 100 days.

Continuous care retirement community

A *continuous care retirement community* (CCRC) is a type of community geared toward providing a gradation of care to older adults, from independent living to assisted living to nursing-home care. The goal of the CCRC is to help older individuals reside in the same community for the remainder of their lives. Such communities tend to be the costliest of all elder-care options, often requiring an upfront sum, as well as monthly charges that will vary depending on the level of care. As with nursing homes and assisted living facilities, most of the care provided within CCRCs is not covered by Medicare, unless it's medical care or skilled nursing care that is normally covered by Medicare. The financial arrangements of CCRCs can be complex.

Custodial care

Custodial care is nonmedical care provided to assist older adults with the activities of daily living. As a rule, custodial care alone is not covered by Medicare; instead, such costs must be covered out of pocket, with long-term care insurance, or by Medicaid for eligible individuals.

Assisted living facility

An assisted living facility is geared toward people who need assistance with the activities of daily living but who do not need the type of extensive care provided in a nursing home. Most assisted living facilities, like nursing homes, help patients coordinate medical care, but providing medical care to sick individuals is not the central focus. Many assisted living facilities now have locked memory care units geared toward people with Alzheimer's disease or dementia. As with nursing homes, stays in assisted living facilities are not covered by Medicare; instead, such care is covered out of pocket or by long-term care insurance.

Nursing home

A nursing home helps individuals with the activities of daily living, including eating, bathing, and getting dressed. Nursing homes are also likely to coordinate or provide medical care for their residents. Unlike skilled nursing facilities, nursing-home care (sometimes called *custodial care*) is not covered by Medicare. Instead, your costs are covered out of pocket, by long-term care insurance, or by Medicaid for individuals with limited assets.

Palliative care

Palliative care provides pain relief and emotional support to individuals with serious illnesses. In contrast to hospice care, which is for terminally ill patients, palliative care can be provided to individuals undergoing curative treatment. Medicare Part B may cover some of the prescriptions and treatments offered under the umbrella of palliative care.

Hospice care

Hospice care is for individuals at the end of their lives; the focus is on keeping the patient comfortable rather than extending life. Such care may be provided at home, in the hospital, or in a skilled nursing facility. Hospice care is covered by Medicare if your doctor and the hospice director certify that you're terminally ill and have less than six months to live. To be covered by Medicare, hospice care cannot be delivered in conjunction with any curative treatment.

Long-term care insurance provides coverage to pay the costs of services such as nursing home, in-home care, and skilled nursing facilities that are not covered by Medicare or Medicare supplements. These costs are quite high—hundreds of dollars a day. Long-term care insurance is like any other type of insurance: It allows you to protect against a potential risk by providing valuable leverage in terms of the premium compared with the total pool of benefits (how much you could get back in claims).

How much long-term care insurance do I need?

The amount of long-term care insurance you will need depends on whether you can go without insurance (self-insure), as well as how much the daily cost of care will be where you live. To see what the average cost of care in your area is for various services, visit the Genworth Cost of Care survey page at https://www.genworth.com/about-us/industry-expertise/cost-of-care.html. Take a look at what you may need and what assets you have, and balance them with a premium you can afford. Keep in mind that long-term care insurance premiums can increase over time, as do premiums for all other types of insurance, including auto insurance, homeowner's insurance, and health insurance.

When you buy a long-term care insurance policy, you'll need to estimate how much care you anticipate needing and for how long. On average, people require about three years of long-term care. You need to weigh the cost of the premium you can pay against what you expect to need from the policy. You'll pay a higher premium for a long-term care policy covering five years of care than you will for a policy that covers just three years. You need to seriously consider that balancing act before you purchase this type of insurance. You don't want to be insurance rich and cash poor.

How should I design my policy?

Long-term care insurance allows you to design your policy to meet your needs through your choice of components, which can vary in definition from company to company. When you are comparison shopping, pay attention to the policy design to get as close as possible to an apples-to-apples comparison. Here are some of the common components:

Maximum daily (or monthly) benefit

This is the maximum specified dollar amount that will be paid on a daily (or monthly) basis for services covered under a policy. Research facilities and services in the area you plan to live during retirement to find out the current daily cost of care.

Elimination period

This is the number of days that you must pay for covered services before the insurance company will make payments (also known as a *waiting period* and comparable to a deductible). Policies can have different elimination periods; most are currently 90 days. Consider that you will need to come up with money out of pocket during this period.

Benefit period

This is the number of days for which benefits will be paid (this can also be expressed as years). Most current policies allow you to carry over unused benefits. For example, if you are using half of your daily maximum benefit, your benefit period would be twice as long.

Inflation rider

An inflation rider increases your benefit to keep pace with inflationary increases in the cost of long-term care.

Shared care (for spouses or partners)

A number of companies offer policies where spouses can use benefits from the other spouse's pool of benefits once their own is exhausted.

Other riders

Other common riders are assisted living benefits, coordination of care, non-forfeiture benefit, restoration of other benefits, and survivorship benefits.

Type of benefit payment

Benefits can be either indemnity, where the policy owner receives the specified benefit amount for covered services even if the cost of services is less than the benefit amount, or cash reimbursement. The reimbursement method pays for the exact amount of expenses (up to the benefit limit); however, payment can be delayed because expenses must be incurred and receipts must be submitted. Payments sometimes can only be made to the care provider. Premiums for reimbursement policies are less, because the claims are usually smaller. Paying the extra premium for an indemnity policy to receive a potential extra benefit is most likely not a good use of funds. Most current policies are reimbursement only, while some are a mix.

TIP

Determine if the policy pays on an indemnity basis (a specified amount to the policyholder up to a daily maximum or monthly maximum regardless of the actual cost of care). If $150 in daily medical charges is incurred and the policy has a $200 daily pay-out, the insured can use the extra $50 for any qualifying expenses. The other form is a reimbursement for covered services.

HOW DO I OPTIMIZE MY PREMIUM?

Check to see if you are eligible for any discounts. The most common discounts are for preferred health and for married couples, couples that share a child, and domestic partners.

Every long-term care insurance policy has certain core definitions and parameters, which can differ from company to company. Long-term care policies allow you to customize the various components to fit your needs and budget. It's important to understand each of these components and whether they fit your financial plan. It is likely that you may need to compromise on benefits to find a policy that will fit within your budget.

WHAT SHOULD I KNOW ABOUT GROUP LONG-TERM CARE INSURANCE?

This is usually offered only through large employers to employees and their spouses. Group long-term care insurance usually has a simplified underwriting process. The policies will also have fewer choices, such as for the daily benefit, benefit period, inflation protection, and other riders. The policies can be discounted to increase participation. Pricing is sometimes based on age bands, so it will increase at certain ages. Premiums can be repriced if you leave the employer or if the insurance company increases the premiums.

WHAT ARE NONTRADITIONAL LONG-TERM CARE INSURANCE OPTIONS?

The big trend currently is for long-term care insurance to be included as part of another insurance policy, either as a hybrid/combination policy or as rider to a life insurance or annuity contract. The concept is that you will accumulate a cash value and gain a death benefit, so that if you do not make a long-term care insurance claim, you may still receive a benefit of some sort. Insurance companies have not been profitable selling stand-alone insurance policies, so these policies were created to offset those lower sales.

The following are the most common types of hybrid/combination long-term care policies and riders:

Life insurance combined with long-term care insurance

Usually funded with a single lump sum premium, a few policies do allow you to spread out premiums over a limited period of time. This combination provides a specified benefit and usually has a cash value equal to the premium. Any long-term care benefits are deducted from the cash value and death benefit, and the long-term care cost may be guaranteed.

Annuity combined with long-term care insurance

This type of contract is also usually funded with a single lump sum premium, and it also provides a specified benefit. There may be a small short-term surrender charge; however, the costs are guaranteed. These contracts may feature simplified underwriting, which allows for clients with poor health (higher risk) to obtain coverage.

Life insurance policy with a long-term care insurance rider

In this case, premium payments can be made over the lifetime of the policy, over a certain number of years, or by lump sum. There is usually no return of premium option, and you are subject to all of the potential issues of a stand-alone cash value life insurance policy. This rider allows for a certain percentage of the death benefit to be used for long-term care costs, but the reimbursement terms can be more stringent than with a traditional long-term care policy or with a hybrid policy.

Annuities with long-term care insurance riders

This type is typically funded with a single premium, and the terms are similar to a fixed annuity. Extra costs may or may not be incurred for the long-term care component, since it's funded by the annuity premium.

Two funds are created in the annuity: The first is for long-term care expenses, and the other is for whatever you choose. The annuity will have specific terms on how much can be withdrawn from each fund. The tax consequences can be complex, coupled with the fact that annuities themselves are complex.

WHY SHOULD I NOT CONSIDER A HYBRID/ COMBINATION LONG-TERM CARE POLICY?

I recommend avoiding hybrid policies. They tend to entail more risk to you and have the following drawbacks.

They get away from the principle of protecting against an uncertain risk

There is no expectation that you receive anything back on your auto, homeowner's, or other types of insurance if you do not make a claim. The point of insurance is to protect you, not pay you for not protecting you.

You may not need a life insurance policy or an annuity

At the age where you are considering long-term care insurance, you are most likely past the age where you will need life insurance, yet you will incur the costs of a life insurance policy with that type of hybrid. Annuities make sense only for a limited percentage of people and have high costs and other restrictions. Remember the overarching theme of this book: Buy only the insurance you actually need.

Regulatory protection

Individual long-term insurance policy premiums are covered in most states by rate stabilization rules, but with hybrid/combination policies and long-term care riders, there is no restriction on the insurance company changing one or more of the policy's pricing components without disclosing it or seeking approval from the state insurance department (in all but nine states), even though the long-term care cost itself may be guaranteed.

Complexity and opacity

Hybrid/combination policies and policies with long-term care riders are complex, have various pricing components, and are not transparent. As noted above, you will usually not know if a pricing component on one of these policies has been changed.

Policies can require a single lump sum premium payment

Why pay for something up front when you can spread out the cost over a number of years? If you have a claim early on, you've already paid for years and years of premiums that you would not have needed to pay. You've also lost the use of these funds for other investing purposes. With most contracts, there will be high surrender charges for the first few years, so you've also lost liquidity.

Risk of losing out on long-term returns

If interest rates increase, the insurance company is not obligated to increase the credited rate on any policy. Some policies have minimal if any contractually guaranteed interest rates. The policies may have a guaranteed death benefit, a long-term care benefit, and a return of premium with no increase in value. That means that the insurance company can profit for years on investing your money before they have to ever pay you anything through a long-term care claim, cash value withdrawal, policy surrender, or death benefit.

No track history

Insurance companies currently have issues with long-term care insurance policies not being priced correctly, with seeking out rate increases, and with failing universal life policies.

You should only consider a hybrid-combination policy if you have another cash value life insurance policy or annuity contract with a significant taxable gain that could be used to fund the combination contract. You would still need to consider whether you are better off surrendering that contract, paying the tax due, investing the money, and then using the income stream to pay for an individual life insurance policy.

HOW DO I APPLY FOR LONG-TERM CARE INSURANCE?

Once you've decided that you would like to apply for long-term care insurance, you'll go through the underwriting process. The process is similar to other types of health insurance. First, you do your research, choose a policy, and complete the application. You may have a phone or even a face-to-face interview with a cognitive test. For example, the examiner may use a ten-word recall segment, where you'll need to recall those words later in the interview.

You may also have a paramedical exam, with blood tests and urine specimens. This can be combined with the face-to-face interview. The most common conditions that insurance companies will test for are cardiovascular risk factors such as high cholesterol and high triglycerides, liver function, kidney function, illegal drugs, HIV, and diabetes (sugar level, A1C level).

HOW DO I MONITOR PERFORMANCE?

Review your policy to confirm what types of care are covered. Many older long-term care policies did not pay for any type of home care or relatively newer types of care like adult day care. It is extremely unlikely that you will be able to replace an existing long-term care insurance policy, because new policies have significantly higher premiums than older policies. The trade-off of extra benefits for additional premiums is almost never worth it.

What about rising long-term care insurance premiums?

If you have been following long-term care insurance, you've heard that premiums on in-force long-term care insurance policies have been increasing significantly. This is partially true; some older policies had significant premiums, and some newer policies have had minimal, if any, premium increases.

In the majority of states, insurance companies must request a rate increase from the state insurance department due to the National Association of Insurance Commissioners Long-Term Care Insurance Model Act. To have a request granted, insurance companies must meet certain maximum profit guidelines (they must usually reduce them, never increase them) and 100 percent of the rate increase must go toward claims and customer service. In other words, insurance companies must prove that they need the premium increase. And it is in your best interest for an insurance company to have a rate increase approved if it is justified, because it will keep your insurance company in business and able to pay necessary claims.

What factors cause premium increases?

Long-term care insurance premiums are based on multiple fluctuating factors. In the prolonged historically low-interest-rate environment, insurance companies have not been able to make their historical investment returns. Insurance companies also counted on a certain percentage of people lapsing (terminating) their policies at some point—around 5 percent—however, that hasn't happened. They made this prediction without much historical data. And guess what? Policy owners actually liked and valued the coverage they purchased, and they have kept their long-term care insurance policies in force, despite some significant rate increases, with actual lapse rates of only 1 percent. Insurance reserve requirements have also increased; this means the companies are required to set aside additional funds to pay future claims. Health care and long-term care costs continue to increase; the average annualized increase in US nursing home costs from 2016–2022 is projected to be 6.3 percent, according to the Center for Medicare Services. Finally, we're all living longer. This extends claims with unlimited benefit periods.

Premiums have had to be increased because, at the end of the day, it is in everyone's best interest for insurance companies to be profitable. If they're not, they will go out of business and will not be able to pay claims, which is a larger problem than higher premiums.

Is there oversight on premium increases?

Premium increases on long-term care insurance policies have to be approved in most states by the state insurance commissioner. When faced with a rate increase, policyholders will need to consider whether their benefit mix makes sense and fits their budget.

These are the visible rate increases, but there are also hidden increases. If you have a long-term care insurance policy with a mutual insurance company where the premium is subsidized by dividends, you may not have noticed (or been informed) of a reduced dividend scale. When an insurance company reduces its dividend scale, it does not have to get approval from anyone or disclose that it has reduced its dividends. Reduced dividends mean a higher premium.

Policies issued today have significantly higher premiums than those issued in the past. Some rate increases are attributed to companies "catching up" on premiums to get closer to current premiums they hope are more accurate. The closer that pricing gets, the less likely it is there will be future premium increases. So if you have an older policy (even if you're faced with a significant premium increase), keep in mind that you've gotten a discount on past premiums. While that's not comforting in the face of a premium increase, it will help put things into perspective.

Insurance departments approve premium increases sufficient to meet anticipated claims. Any increase must apply equally to all policy owners from a class of policies, and the carrier must keep the policy in force if the premium payments are made. Changes in age or health have no bearing on the contract premiums once a policy is issued; policies may only be canceled if premiums are not paid. Nearly all existing long-term care insurance policies have had one or more rate increases granted by the state.

Please keep in mind that rates on other types of insurance also increase over the years, some slowly like auto insurance and homeowner's insurance and some rapidly like health insurance. Inflation affects everything. There are no nickel candy bars anymore. This is all about the value of the coverage and the leverage of your premium to the total benefit pool.

What are my options if my long-term care insurance premium is increased?

When you have a premium increase, you should always start by reviewing your coverage and deciding whether you still need the current coverage or whether you can make changes. For example, because the average claim period is two to three years and there is a much longer benefit period, consider whether the trade-off in premiums for the longer benefit period is worth it. It is important to understand that, once a change is made it cannot be undone, so be sure you are comfortable with any modifications.

You have several options when your premium increases. You can simply pay the increased premium if you can still afford it and the coverage still meets your needs. You can reduce the daily/monthly benefit amount, increase the waiting period, or shorten the benefit period. You can change the inflation rider (e.g., go from compound to simple or reduce inflation percentage from 5 percent to 4 percent), or you can change or remove other riders. Finally, you can terminate the policy. If your policy has a nonforfeiture benefit that allows for a *paid-up reduced benefit*, consider this last option. You'll get at least some value for the premiums you've paid. But remember, once you cancel the policy, it will not be reinstated. Although it's relatively rare in older policies, some states are now requiring all new policies to include this feature.

HOW DO I FILE A CLAIM?

A long-term care insurance policy will typically pay a benefit if there is a significant cognitive impairment or when you cannot perform a certain number of the activities of daily living; on current policies, it's two out of six; however, on older policies, it may be different. The following are the covered activities of daily living used to measure a disabled or elderly individual's level of functioning:

- Bathing
- Dressing
- Eating
- Ambulating/transferring (moving from place to place or from standing position to chair)
- Continence
- Toileting

WHAT IS SHORT-TERM CARE INSURANCE?

Short-term care insurance is a new form of critical care insurance that functions much like long-term care insurance. These policies are also known as *recovery insurance*. The maximum coverage period is typically one year, although many policies only have maximum benefit periods of three to six months. This coverage has gained popularity, since about 50 percent of all long-term care insurance claims are for less than a year. These policies can also be easier to qualify for and typically only consist of yes or no health questions.

The policies pay claims based on the same eligibility for a long-term care insurance claim, when you need assistance with two or more activities of daily living. There is generally no elimination period. Benefits can be extended if the full benefit is not used, similar to long-term care insurance. Short-term care can also be used to offset long-term care expenses during Medicare's waiting period or a long-term care policy's waiting period.

Given the limited benefits, short-term care insurance policies rarely make sense. Short-term care insurance policies are not subject to the same regulatory standards as long-term care insurance, such as rate stabilization rules. Therefore, insurance companies can increase premiums without regulatory approval.

CHAPTER 9

Annuities: Selecting Your Punter

"When you have a problem,
rules don't solve your problem.
It's caring and education."

—JIM BROWN

J im Brown is among the greatest football players in the history of the NFL. He made the Pro Bowl (NFL all-star team) every year he played, and when he retired, he held almost every NFL rushing record, while only having played nine seasons, and he was soon added to the NFL Hall of Fame. Brown was known for his hard work, toughness, and dedication.

Brown recognizes, in his quote above, that education is more important than simply having rules. This means that rules can help you; however, it takes understanding and thinking to be successful. Annuities are a complex area and have a lot of rules. The value of annuities is widely questioned, as most annuities do not provide the value that they should.

The value of a punter is often misunderstood or even overlooked. While punters only play a small percentage of the game, a great punter can be a huge factor in its outcome. The key is that punters are specialized players, just as annuities are specialized insurance contracts. Annuities should be used only when needed and only for insurance—rather than investment—purposes.

An annuity is a contract between you and an insurance company that requires the company to make payments to you, either immediately or in the future. You buy an annuity by making either a single payment or a series of payments. Similarly, your payout may come either as one lump sum payment or as a series of payments over time.

DO I NEED AN ANNUITY?

Annuities are helpful if you have a specific need that cannot be fulfilled through another product. The most common reason to use annuities is for periodic payments for a specified amount of time (this can be for the rest of your life, for the life of your spouse or another person, or for a set number of years). Annuities are a good solution for someone who has issues with spending their savings. Purchasing an annuity will "lock up" their money and allow them to receive a guaranteed income. When you compare an annuity to other investments, you will find higher fees and surrender charges that, over the long run, will most likely cost you more and result in lower accumulated funds.

Using an annuity to create a predictable income stream provides the following benefits:

A steady and predictable income

Annuities turn a lump sum into a fixed monthly payment that can be used to offset monthly expenses. Basically, it removes the uncertainty of having to withdraw from your other assets when the market is volatile. Withdrawal planning is a challenging part of retirement planning.

Offsetting longevity risk

Longevity risk is the risk that a retiree will outlive their investment portfolio. A financial contract that will always pay back a set amount each month for as long as you live is something that is well worth considering. As we continue to live longer, outliving your money is a real risk.

Transfer market risk to the insurance company

Since the annuity pays out a certain amount, you will not be affected by the volatility of the stock and bond markets. This is especially helpful during a bear market, since you would have less of a need to take withdrawals from other assets.

Removes the need to actively manage some of your investments

As you age, you may have less interest or cognitive capacity to manage your investment accounts and maintain a withdrawal plan. An annuity simplifies your withdrawals.

Your principal is protected

Since you transfer your money to the insurance company, they are responsible for it.

Annuities are also useful for when someone's spending needs to be restricted. For example, if you are leaving money to someone who cannot handle their own financial affairs well or who might be at risk for losing the money, annuities allow the money to be protected if the annuity is set to pay out.

Keep in mind that annuities are, by nature, a conservative product and should only be used for their intended purpose of transferring risk to the insurance company. Don't become blinded by policy features that are hard to understand and high in fees.

TIP

A common selling point is that annuities usually feature tax-deferred growth on the income and investment gains until money is withdrawn. That's true under current tax law. However, current tax law is not guaranteed, and if the law is changed, there will be no recourse for annuity owners. Purchasing any type of financial product solely for tax reasons is usually not a good idea.

WHAT SHOULD I LOOK FOR IN AN ANNUITY?

If you feel that an annuity is the right investment choice for you, you can purchase one either as an immediate annuity, where the annuitant (you) receives benefits immediately, or as a deferred annuity, where the benefits are deferred until a later date. Here is where you can easily go off the rails with all the different choices of annuities and wide array of riders. We'll review the more common ones over the next pages. Just keep in mind that you should never purchase any type of financial services product that you don't understand well enough to explain to someone else.

What are the basic phases of an annuity?

Annuities have two basic phases. In the *accumulation phase*, your payments are made into the annuity and accumulate based on the type of annuity. Interest accumulates on a tax-deferred basis. In the *payout phase*, you receive your payments back, along with any investment income and gains.

What are common annuity classifications?

Annuities are classified in a number of ways. The two most common classifications are deferred and immediate. In a *deferred annuity*, the payment of proceeds is put off (deferred) to a future time—5, 10, or 15 years after the money is put into the annuity. In an *immediate annuity*, as you might have guessed, a lump sum of money is put into the annuity, and the annuity immediately begins making a series of payments. Note that once the 30-day free look period is over, you are usually locked in and cannot make any changes or access your principal.

How do I fund an annuity?

Annuities are also often classified by the manner and method in which the premium payments are made. With *single premium annuities*, you make a single one-time cash contribution; no further contributions are allowed. Note that immediate or income annuities are always single premium. With *flexible premium annuities*, you can make multiple contributions into the annuity policy at different times. These contributions (along with other factors, such as the crediting method, policy expenses, annuitization options, and surrender charges) will affect how much the policy pays out.

What are the different types of annuities?

There are many different types of annuities, typically classified by the way interest is credited. The most common types of annuities are listed here:

Fixed annuity

Fixed annuities feature a minimum rate of interest, which is declared annually by the insurance company and is payable for a specified number of years. These are the most stable and conservative type of annuities and tend to pay lower rates of interest.

Indexed annuity

Also known as *fixed-indexed* (FIA) or *equity-indexed annuities* (EIA), indexed annuities combine features of securities and insurance products. The insurance company credits you with a return that is based on a stock market index, such as the Standard & Poor's 500 Index. The value of an indexed annuity will vary with the movements of the chosen index (note that you are not actually investing in the index). Usually there is a guaranteed rate of return of 0 percent, so that you don't have a loss in any year. These annuities can be volatile and theoretically provide a higher return than a fixed annuity; however, this return can be restricted by the company, and these policies can have high surrender charges, long surrender periods, and other stringent withdrawal limitations. Insurance companies can also change the administrative fee, along with the following components on a periodic basis—usually annually:

Interest rate (earnings) cap

This is a cap on the maximum return that can be earned on an annuity. For example, an annuity may have a 5-percent cap; even if the market returns more than 5 percent, you would receive just the 5 percent.

Participation rate

This is amount of the return that you will receive. The participation rate is usually 100 percent; however, the insurance company can change this. For example, if your participation rate is 75 percent and the annuity returns 5 percent, you would receive only 3.5 percent (5% × 75%). Remember, this is net of the cap, so if the index return is 10 percent, you would still only receive 3.5 percent.

Spread

There may also be a spread, or margin, in addition or in place of the participation rate, and it would work the same way. In the case of an annuity with a spread of 3 percent, if the index gained 6 percent, the return credited to the annuity would be 3 percent (6% − 3% = 3%).

Indexing Method

Another feature that can have a dramatic impact on an indexed annuity's return is its indexing method (or how the amount of change in the relevant index is determined). The amount of change is determined at the end of each crediting period within the contract's accumulation period. In many contracts, the crediting period is one year, although the length of the crediting period may vary from one contract to another. There are different indexing methods, so be sure to review the options available to you. Insurance companies may not credit you with index-linked interest for a crediting period if you do not hold your contract to the end of the period.

Variable annuity

A variable annuity combines features of securities and investment products and allows you to direct payments to different investment options, known as *subaccounts*. The subaccounts are usually mutual funds; however, be aware that although they may share the name of a *mutual fund*, they are not identical. For instance, there is a Vanguard 500 mutual fund used for investing and a separate Vanguard 500 mutual fund used for insurance subaccounts. They may not—in fact, almost surely don't—have the same investment allocation, so the returns and expenses will differ. The value of your annuity will vary depending on how much you put in, the rate of return on your investments, and expense charges such as a mortality and expense risk charge (known as M&E), administrative fees, fund expense ratios for the underlying funds, fees, and charges for other features and riders. The total fees are usually 2–3.5 percent of the contract value each year. Variable annuities also have withdrawal penalties, including surrender charges, and partial withdrawal limitations.

While variable annuities will often be projected to have higher returns than fixed annuities, they lack the guarantees of a fixed annuity and are riskier, even beyond all the fees described above.

Longevity annuities

In *longevity annuities*, also known as *deferred income annuities*, income is deferred until a certain age (usually age 85 and a minimum of one year). Typically, they will offer a higher guaranteed lifetime income at a later date than an immediate annuity. The longer you wait to defer the benefit, the higher it will be. These will have fees, along with surrender charges. There is a downside risk: If you don't live to the deferral age, there is no value in the contract. For example, if you purchase a longevity annuity at age 65 that is deferred to age 80 and you pass away at age 79, you will have received nothing from the contract. (At this point, there will be nothing left for the beneficiaries.)

Variable annuities and indexed annuities are complex financial products with many permutations. These annuities also carry investment risk and potentially very high fees. If you do decide to opt for either of these products, make sure that you fully understand all the risks and fees that are involved.

Where is the interest credited?

It's important to understand where interest is credited. It is often credited only to the income benefit (also known as the *annuitization benefit*) rather than fully to your cash value. Your annuitization benefit will often be different from your cash value. The interest is not credited to the principal. If you decide to terminate the annuity, you would lose some or all of the interest.

What should I know about annuity illustrations?

Illustrations are simply projections; they are not guarantees. Consider how the illustration looks based on a worst-case and an average-case scenario rather than just on current or best-case scenarios. The illustrations will show a steady growth rate; unfortunately, the market does not move at a steady rate (either up or down) but in a more volatile fashion. What this means is that the illustration will not provide you with your true return, as it doesn't reflect the variance.

What are common annuity riders?

Riders are very popular on annuity contracts, and there are many of them out there. The riders may not be the same from company to company. Be aware that while the names of different riders may be similar, the way the riders work may be very different. Riders are generally complex and can come at a high cost. While they do provide guarantees on income payments, they come at a cost. Here is a list of some of the most common riders:

Guaranteed lifetime withdrawal benefit

This rider guarantees a minimum level of lifetime income. If the portfolio's value rises, your income can rise. The annual fees for this rider are approximately 1 percent of the assets under management.

Guaranteed lifetime withdrawal benefit

The GLWB guarantees that a certain percentage (typically 3–5 percent, often based on age) of the amount invested can be withdrawn each year for as long as the contract holder lives. This percentage may vary depending on the person's age when withdrawals begin, whether the payment is guaranteed to continue for the life of one (single life) or two (joint life) individuals, and in some of the newest structures based on the level of an external benchmark such as the 10-Year Constant Maturity Treasury Rate. In many GLWBs, *step-up* features periodically (e.g., annually or every five years) lock in higher guaranteed withdrawals if investments do well. *Roll-up* features, conversely, increase the amount that may be withdrawn (by increasing the *benefit base* used to calculate withdrawals) during the deferral period (i.e., prior to the commencement of withdrawals). Allocation to a balanced or volatility-managed fund, adherence to an asset allocation program, or a minimum allocation to a fixed or fixed-income subaccount is often required when electing a GLWB.

Guaranteed minimum accumulation benefit

A GMAB rider guarantees that your contract value will be set at least equal to a certain minimum percentage (usually 100 percent) of the amount invested after a specified number of years (typically ten years), regardless of actual investment performance.

Guaranteed minimum income benefit

A GMIB rider is designed to provide a base amount of lifetime income when the contract is annuitized regardless of how the investments have performed. It guarantees that if the owner decides to annuitize the contract (for life, life plus a certain period, or the lives of two people), payments are based on the greater of the contract value or the amount invested, credited with simple or compound interest at a rate of 1–4 percent. The GMIB creates a notional balance on which annuity payments can be calculated; it does not represent account or cash value. You must annuitize to receive this benefit, and there is typically a ten-year holding period before it can be exercised. Age limits may also apply.

Guaranteed minimum withdrawal benefit

A GMWB rider guarantees that a certain percentage (usually 4–6 percent) of the amount invested can be withdrawn annually until the entire amount is recovered, regardless of market performance. Reducing with-drawals in one year generally does not allow for increased withdrawals in subsequent years. However, if you defer withdrawals and the account value grows and is locked in at certain points as the new benefit base, the amount of subsequent withdrawals allowed may be larger.

If the underlying investments perform well, there will be an excess amount in the policy at the end of the withdrawal period. If they per-form poorly and the account value is depleted before the end of the withdrawal period, you can continue to make withdrawals until the full amount of the original investment is recovered. If you decide to ter-minate the contract before the end of the withdrawal period, you will receive the cash surrender value of the contract. A GMWB rider allows minimum withdrawals from the invested amount without having to annuitize the investment.

Income benefit riders (in general)

Insurance companies credit an additional percentage each year prior to taking income. This extra amount can be up to an additional 5–7 per-cent per year. Income riders cease when you begin to take distributions. Remember, this is not credited to your surrender value; it is credited to your income benefit (annuitization benefit), which is used to determine your guaranteed payout.

Long-term care

This rider allows you to withdraw money for long-term care needs with-out incurring surrender charges. Surrender charges may be waived if, for example, you have been confined to a nursing home for a mini-mum period or have suffered a critical illness. Additional benefits may be offered, such as eldercare resources, referral and consultation services, and discounted long-term care services from a specified group of pro-viders. Insurance carriers have also developed true insurance benefits for long-term care, such as riders that double the lifetime withdrawal payment of a GLWB when you are confined to a nursing home.

Stand-alone living benefit

The SALB provides protection similar to that of the GLWB while adding flexibility with the various types of assets that can be protected. It is designed to be attached to a balanced fund by endorsement, primarily for use as an option in an employer-sponsored retirement plan. Development of the market for these products has been slow due to ambiguity around the fiduciary responsibilities of the plan sponsor in selecting an insurance carrier and issues around portability that make it difficult to move the benefit when you change employers.

PENSION PLAN ROLLOVERS

If you are fortunate enough to have a pension program, you may be offered a lump sum, which could be exchanged (on a tax-free basis) to an annuity. Be careful to ensure that your annuity payout would be higher than the pension payout; part of this will depend on the type of payout. Also, depending on the type of annuity, you may face other restrictions on your funds. If you are concerned about the safety of your pension and the company going bankrupt, keep in mind that the US Pension Benefit Guarantee Fund guarantees the pension payouts.

HOW WOULD I RECEIVE MONEY FROM AN ANNUITY?

Annuitization options are the choices an annuity holder has to receive the annuity value other than in a lump sum. As the annuity owner, you can choose how you want the payments to be made. Common annuitization options are listed below.

Life only

Payments stop when the annuity owner dies.

Period certain

The annuity pays out over a specified period of time and stops paying once that time period has elapsed, even if the annuitant is still alive. The typical periods are 5, 10, 15, and 20 years.

Life with period certain

Payments are guaranteed to be made to the annuity owner for as long as the annuitant lives. The payment is also guaranteed for a certain number of years, should the annuitant die early. For example, a *life with ten-year certain* payout would guarantee payments for at least ten years; if the annuitant dies after the first year, the beneficiaries would start receiving the payments, to be paid out over the remaining nine years. On the other hand, if the annuitant is still alive after the ten-year initial period, payments will continue so long as the annuitant lives. (In this case, when the annuitant dies, the payments cease.)

Joint and survivor annuity

Your beneficiary will continue to receive payouts for the rest of their life after the annuitant dies. This is a popular option for married couples.

TIP

Read the details of your contract; it is easy to get locked into an annuity where you cannot liquidate the annuity, and the fees can be excessive.

What is the exclusion ratio?

This formula determines which portion of an annuity payment is considered taxable and which is a tax-free return of principal. For example, if you paid in $50,000 and your earnings were $50,000 for a total annuitization value of $100,000, your ratio would be 50 percent and would be subject to ordinary income tax.

What are surrender charges and withdrawal limitations?

Surrender penalties or *charges* in an annuity are charges that an insurance company deducts from the accumulation value of the policy if money is withdrawn during the surrender period. Each annuity has its own surrender period and charge.

Surrender period

This is a period of time (generally expressed in years) during which penalties will be charged for early withdrawal of money from the policy. Common surrender periods are 5, 6, and 10 years; however, some annuities have very long surrender periods, of 20 years or more.

Surrender charge

This is a percentage amount assessed against the annuity account for early withdrawals of money. Surrender charges work in conjunction with surrender periods. Surrender charges are generally expressed in decreasing percentages as time goes by. For example, an annuity with a ten-year surrender charge might have a 10-percent surrender penalty in the first year, 9 percent in the second year, and so on.

Death benefit

The amount the named beneficiary receives upon death of the annuitant is called the death benefit. The important thing to note here is that some annuities reduce the death benefit by the surrender charge, while others do not.

Bonus recapture

If the contract is surrendered or a partial withdrawal is taken in excess of the free withdrawal limit, a certain percentage of the bonus will be recaptured by the insurance company and therefore lost to you. The bonus recapture is usually shown as a percentage of the amount surrendered associated with the premium bonus. This bonus recapture period can last from five to ten years and starts at 100 percent in the first two years, 80 percent in years three and four, and so on.

Two-tier annuities

Two-tier annuities have two separate cash values: one if the policy is annuitized, another if it is surrendered outright. If a policy is surrendered rather than annuitized, there can be substantial surrender penalties. Conversely, if a two-tier annuity is annuitized, the owner no longer has access to the cash in the annuity. Two-tier annuities are typically very difficult to understand and should be approached with caution.

Withdrawal limitations

Most annuities will allow an annual free withdrawal of a certain amount. Any withdrawal beyond this is subject to a surrender charge (usually 10 percent per year of the principal plus interest earned).

Early withdrawal penalty

Annuity owners generally incur a 10 percent penalty tax on withdrawals of accumulated interest during the accumulation phase prior to age 59½, unless the annuity owner is disabled. This may also apply to the annuitization phase if the annuity was not an immediate annuity and the owner selected certain short payout terms. Annuitization of a deferred annuity during the accumulation phase will be subject to the pre-59½ penalty unless the I.R.C. §72(q)(2)(D) requirements for substantially equal periodic payments are met. Visit my website for more information.

Market value adjustment

A *market value adjustment* (MVA) is a feature included in some annuity contracts that imposes an adjustment or fee when you surrender a fixed annuity or the fixed account of a variable annuity. The adjustment is based on the relationship of market interest rates at the time of surrender and the interest rate guaranteed in the annuity.

Surrender charges vary greatly from annuity to annuity. The higher the surrender charge and the longer the surrender period, the higher the commission the agent is paid on the product. High surrender charges tend to be red flags that an agent is attempting to sell an unsuitable or abusive annuity to a senior. You should pay close attention to the terms of an annuity's surrender penalties.

Annuities are not designed to be used as a source of ready cash. They are not savings or checking accounts, and there can be hefty charges levied against the owner who tries to take money out at a faster rate than the contract allows.

HOW DO I MAXIMIZE VALUE ON AN ANNUITY?

There are literally hundreds of annuities in the marketplace. If you are considering purchasing an annuity, remember that all annuities are not created equal. They can be very complicated and difficult to understand. Do not purchase an annuity until you are absolutely sure that you completely understand how it works and that it makes sense to you. It is always a good idea to get an objective second opinion from a neutral party before you commit to purchasing an annuity. Always keep in mind first and foremost that the consequences of making a bad decision could adversely affect you for the rest of your life.

You should always read all of the documentation provided about the annuity. If you don't understand something, ask questions. If you still don't understand, this is not the product for you.

Money that is put into an annuity is usually locked up for a period specified in the annuity, typically five to ten years. With some annuities, there are permanent limitations on withdrawals. If you withdraw some or all your money during the specified time period, you will have to pay a surrender charge. Annuities are not for short-term goals; they are long-term contracts.

Ask about these surrender charges. Consider if you may be surrendering the annuity prior to the end of the surrender charge period. Typically the surrender charge decreases each year until it goes away (if it does go away), so the closer you are to the end of the time the money must be locked up, the smaller the surrender charge.

Pay attention to optional features offered with annuities, and get information about these features and the additional fees associated with adding benefits. This is where buying an annuity can get tricky.

Use the free look period all annuities have. Read and understand the terms of the contract. If you decide the terms are not favorable, you can cancel the contract and receive all of your money back. This only applies during the free look period, so make sure you know when this period ends.

What's a good strategy for low interest rate environments?

If interest rates are low, you want to consider spreading your purchasing of immediate income annuities over a few years. This allows you to optimally have some annuities paying a higher interest rate, which will increase your annuity's payments. This strategy is called *laddering*.

HOW DO I MONITOR AN ANNUITY?

Here are your options when monitoring your annuity is relatively straightforward. You can do nothing and maintain the annuity; annuitize the contract and begin receiving an income; or surrender (cash in) the annuity, pay tax on the gain, and invest the net proceeds in a taxable account.

Other Types of Insurance: Handling Trick Plays

"It ain't like football;
you can't make up no trick plays."
—YOGI BERRA

A unique part of sports—and especially of football—is the trick play. It's something that's unexpected and high risk/high return, usually with no middle ground. Trick plays often don't work; however, they can be a lot of fun to watch.

Insurance also features many types of trick plays—some ranging from insurance coverages that might be useful in specific situations, while others remain questionable. Most specialized insurance coverages are usually not worth the premiums. Make sure that you have a true need for coverage before you purchase something. Remember that the benefits must be worth the premiums paid.

For example, burial insurance, credit card life insurance, and mortgage life insurance are almost always bad deals. Accidental death and dismemberment insurance is one of the worst buys; instead, consider buying adequate amounts of regular term life insurance and disability insurance for both spouses. That way you're covered whether or not your death or injury is caused by an accident.

The following are common (and not-so-common) other types of insurance:

Accidental death and dismemberment

A type of coverage that pays benefits, sometimes including reimbursement for loss of income, in case of sickness, accidental injury, or accidental death.

Builder risk insurance

Builder risk insurance covers construction exposures beyond the limited parameters of a standard commercial property insurance policy. This can be added on as an additional policy or endorsements.

Burial insurance

Burial insurance is a type of life insurance paid out on death to cover final expenses such as the cost of a funeral.

Credit insurance

Credit insurance is offered by lenders when you take out a loan and protects you in the event of a death, disability, or unemployment to pay either the monthly payments or the total balance. Make sure that you understand what is paid; some coverage only pays monthly payments and may have a waiting period of 14–30 days.

Critical illness insurance

Critical illness insurance pays a benefit if you have a qualifying major illness. Each policy has its own list of covered illnesses. If you are diagnosed with one of these illnesses while you're a policyholder, your insurer will typically pay you a lump sum cash payment. The following are examples of illnesses that might be covered: Alzheimer's disease, cancer, and stroke. Critical illness insurance is not health care insurance, disability income insurance, life insurance, or long-term care insurance and does not provide the same benefits.

Directors and officers liability insurance

Directors and officers liability insurance covers directors and officers for claims made against them while serving on a board of directors or as an officer. D&O liability insurance can be written to cover the directors and officers of for-profit businesses, privately held firms, not-for-profit organizations, and educational institutions.

General liability insurance

General liability insurance is a type of business insurance that protects you from damage done to someone else's property by your operations, as well as injuries sustained at your place of business.

Identity insurance

Identity insurance provides protection for businesses that suffer a data breach. It may also cover the costs of notifying and providing services to victims of identity theft.

Identity theft insurance

Identity theft insurance provides limited protection in the event of identity theft. Coverage includes the cost of reclaiming your financial identity, including making phone calls, making copies, mailing documents, taking time off from work without pay, and hiring an attorney. It does not cover your direct financial losses.

International health care insurance

International health care insurance provides health coverage no matter where you are in the world. The policy term is flexible, so you can purchase it only for the time you will be out of the country.

Liability insurance

Liability insurance provides coverage for your obligations and legal defense for accidents, injuries, and negligence. Home-based businesses need liability coverage, since homeowner's policies do not provide protection against business liability risks.

Pet insurance

Pet insurance, also known as *pet health insurance*, provides coverage for your dog or cat in the event of unexpected health issues. There are three main types of coverage: accident only, accident and illness, and wellness and routine care. Coverage is not the same as health insurance and does not cover everything. It's important to read the policy to make sure you get the coverage you are looking for and so you don't have any surprises.

Private mortgage insurance

Private mortgage insurance insures the lender against default by the borrower. This is required by mortgage lenders when you are unable to make a down payment or have equity that is less than 20 percent of your home's total value. Coverage may be through a private insurance company or, if your mortgage is issued through a government program, a designated federal agency. You do not have the right to choose a mortgage insurer; they are chosen by your lender. You do have the right to ask your lender to find you the lowest PMI premium available.

Product liability insurance

Product liability insurance provides coverage for manufacturers, wholesalers, distributors, and resellers from being held liable if a product is unsafe or injures someone.

Professional liability

Professional liability (also known as *errors and omissions [E&O] insurance*) provides coverage for in-service occupations such as attorneys, physicians, accountants, financial planners, and insurance agents from liability for negligence or malpractice in performing their professional duties. It's important to note if your policy is written on a *claims-made and reported basis*, which requires claims to be made and reported during the applicable policy period. Most policies do offer an extended reporting period, which is important because it allows the insured extra time to report a claim after the policy has expired. Details are important on these policies, so read your agreement carefully.

Property insurance

Property insurance provides protection if your property is damaged or destroyed due to fire, storm, or theft. For home-based businesses, your homeowner's policy may provide protection for your business property, or you may be able to add a rider rather than getting a separate policy. There are two forms: standard, and special—which provides more comprehensive coverage.

Reinsurance

Reinsurance is a type of insurance purchased by insurance companies or self-insured employers to protect against unexpected losses

Title insurance

Title insurance provides a guarantee that a title to real property is vested in the purchaser or mortgagee, free and clear of liens or encumbrances. It is usually issued in conjunction with a search of the public records performed at the time of a real estate transaction.

Travel insurance

Travel insurance protects you when traveling abroad by providing coverage for certain losses, such as medical expenses, loss of personal belongings, travel delay, and personal liabilities. Different types of coverage are available for medical events and terrorism. It can provide coverage if you or a family member suffer an injury or illness that prevents you from traveling or that interrupts a trip. It can reimburse you for medical expenses while you travel but will typically not cover an existing medical condition. Review your existing health insurance coverage to see if it will cover medical expenses outside the United States.

About a third of all credit cards offer trip cancellation coverage and lost luggage coverage. You should comparison shop, as travel insurance can be expensive. Be sure to read the fine print on what triggers coverage. You should also avoid *cancel for any reason* coverage, as this can add as much as 40 percent or more to the cost of basic coverage while often paying out only 75 percent of your costs or reimbursing you with future travel credits rather than cash.

Terrorism insurance

Terrorism insurance provides coverage to individuals and businesses for potential losses due to acts of terrorism. For individuals, homeowner's insurance, condominium insurance, renter's insurance, life insurance, and auto insurance policies with comprehensive coverage already cover terrorist attacks. Disability insurance and health insurance policies may also provide coverage. Businesses usually have to purchase terrorism coverage separately at a price that reflects the current risk.

Index

equity-indexed universal life (EIUL)
insurance, 178–79
errors and omissions (E&O) insurance,
60, 234–35
exclusion ratio, 226–27
exclusive provider organizations (EPOs),
123
explanation of benefits (EOB), 132
extended/transition benefit, 102–3

F

fairness, 23–29
fake injury claims, 88
family car available for regular use, 90
Federal Employees Dental and Vision
Insurance Program (FEDVIP), 62
Federal Employees' Group Life Insurance
Program (FEGLI), 62–63
Federal Employees Health Benefits
(FEHB) Program, 62–63
Federal Health Care Exchange, 120
Federal Long-Term Care Insurance
Program (FLTCIP), 63
FEDVIP (Federal Employees Dental and
Vision Insurance Program), 62
FEGLI (Federal Employees' Group Life
Insurance Program), 62–63
FEHB (Federal Employees Health
Benefits) Program, 62–63
FINRA, 29
FIO (future increase option), 101–2,
106–7
Fitch rating agency, 18
fixed annuities, 219
fixed-indexed annuities (FIA), 219–20
flexible premium annuities, 218–19
flexible premium (universal) life
insurance, 177
flexible spending accounts (FSAs), 63–64,
134

flood insurance, 161–64
FLTCIP (Federal Long-Term Care
Insurance Program), 63
formularies, 115–16
for sale (rogue) designations, 15
FPO (future purchase option), 101–2,
106–7
fraud, 39–41
auto insurance, 83, 88–89
defined, 40
elder fraud, 66
hard insurance fraud, 41
homeowner's/renter's insurance, 157
life insurance, 181
Medicare, 146
soft insurance fraud, 41
fraudulent car repairs, 88
Fry, Hayden, 5
FSAs (flexible spending accounts), 63–64,
134
future increase option (FIO), 101–2,
106–7
future purchase option (FPO), 101–2,
106–7

G

gap insurance, 133
general liability insurance, 233
Genworth Cost of Care survey, 202
Gibbs, Joe, 1
GLWB (guaranteed lifetime withdrawal
benefit), 222–23
GMAB (guaranteed minimum
accumulation benefit), 223
GMIB (guaranteed minimum income
benefit), 223
GMWB (guaranteed minimum
withdrawal benefit), 223–24
graded death benefit life insurance, 184
grandfathered plans, 118–19

A Note from the Author

Dear Reader,

Thank you for taking the time to learn about how different types of insurance fit into your financial life. I hope you are feeling more in control of your insurance and ready to implement your optimal insurance portfolio with *Insurance Made Easy*.

If you loved the book and have a minute to spare, I would really appreciate a short review on your favorite book site. You're the reason why I continue to write about financial preparedness and advocate for integrity in financial services.

If you think this book might help others to better understand insurance, feel free to invite them to take a complimentary Financial Preparedness Quiz at www.tonysteuer.com. They'll receive a Financial Preparedness Score with a customized to-do list, including reviewing their life insurance and monthly email tips to show them how they can become financially prepared.

So, what's next? Stay up-to-date on the latest in financial preparedness by subscribing to the GET READY! newsletter and the Staying Ready newsletter at www.tonysteuer.com. A paid subscription to Staying Ready provides monthly reminders on important financial to-dos, offers clear and simple checklists to help you accomplish these to-dos, and gives you access to downloadable PDFs for keeping your GET READY! planner and binder current. Financial preparedness is a life-long journey. Join our community, and I'll help you along the way.

Thank you!

Tony

About the Author

When life decides it's time for a crisis, it's likely most of us are unprepared. My greatest passion is to help you GET READY! for those life changing events by showing you how to create and maintain a financial first aid kit and become financially prepared.

I'm a teacher with a sense of humor.

I love helping others makes sense of the financial world in way that is easy to understand. I get that we all don't speak insurance-ese or financial-ese. As a financial guy with a knack for writing, my goal is to guide you through the insurance and financial worlds using language and laughs that everyone can understand. As a result, my first book, *Questions and Answers on Life Insurance*, was born in 2004 and opened up a new path for financial literacy.

Since then, book writing has led to many media interviews, guest articles, and the launch of the Insurance Literacy Movement and the Financial Integrity Pledge, designed to protect your financial interests.

I love learning.

The world of finances and insurance is always changing (e.g., new president = new health care). Stick with me, and I'll keep you on top of the financial and insurance worlds. Being financially and insurance organized was a must when my young son was diagnosed with Type 1 diabetes a few years ago. I learned how to access resources for my son.

When I'm not helping others GET READY!, you might find me cheering on the Warriors with the latest IPA, playing basketball with my friends, enjoying some Grateful Dead tunes, or reading a great mystery or history book. My greatest joy is being Cheryl's husband and Avery's dad.

My goal is to always treat you with respect and to help guide you to make the best insurance-related decisions for your needs. Running a business with integrity is important to me.

So, let's stay connected. Visit tonysteuer.com to learn your financial preparedness score, sign up for the GET READY! newsletter, download checklists, and join the community discussion.

Looking forward to helping you GET READY!

Tony

THE OFFICIAL BIO

Tony Steuer has led the way in establishing a path for financial preparedness through his award winning books:

*Insurance Made Easy**

*Questions and Answers on Life Insurance: The Life Insurance Toolbook*** ****

*The Questions and Answers on Life Insurance Workbook**

The Questions and Answers on Disability Insurance Workbook

The Questions and Answers on Insurance Planner

GET READY!

    *Awarded the Apex Award for Publication

    **Awarded the Excellence in Financial Literacy Education (EIFLE) Award from the Institute of Financial Literacy

    ***Named as one of the top Nine Great Investment Books Worth Reading by *Forbes*

Tony regularly consults with InsureTechs, financial planners, insurance agencies, attorneys, insurance companies, and other financial service companies on insurance marketing and product best practices and on strategies to help consumers GET READY! through financial preparedness and the Financial Integrity Pledge. Tony is a past member of the California Department of Insurance Curriculum Board and current member of the National Financial Educator's Council (NFEC) Curriculum Advisory Board.

He is regularly featured in the media. Tony has appeared in interviews for the *New York Times*, the *Washington Post, U.S. News & World Report*, Slate.com, BottomLine Personal, BankRate.com, Insure .com, InsuranceQuotes.com, Mint.com, You and Your Family, and BenefitsPro. com. He has appeared as a guest on the *Wall Street Journal Morning Radio Show, Prudent Money Show, Your Financial Editor, Insider Secrets, Suzy G. in the Morning Show*, *Financial Finesse*, GrowingMoney.com, Nolo.com, TheNest .com, LovetoKnow.com, and LifeInsuranceSelling.com. Tony also served as a technical editor for *The Retirement Bible* and *The Investing Bible*.

He is passionate about giving back. Tony is involved with many worthwhile causes, including Diabetes Youth Families (board member), Alameda Community Learning Center (board member), Creative Community Education Foundation (Treasurer), and St. Joseph's Elementary School (former school advisory board member), and he is a member of the Lucille Packard Children's Hospital Foundation Advisory Council. Tony has also been a coach for his son's Catholic Youth Organization Basketball team and Little League Baseball team, taught wilderness first aid and white-water rescue, volunteered as a white-water raft guide, and performed improvisational comedy.

Tony Steuer lives in Alameda, California.